CELEBRATIONS

RECIPES FOR FESTIVE OCCASIONS

The author

Simone Sekers is the author of several cookery books, including *Effortless Entertaining* (Piatkus Books), *Fine Foods* (Hodder), *Quick and Easy Preserves* (BBC Books) and *The National Trust Book of Fruit and Vegetable Cookery* (National Trust). She has written a regular cookery column for the *Daily Telegraph* and the *Sunday Telegraph*, and has also contributed to *Country Life* and *Country Homes and Interiors*. She lives in Surrey, enjoys food shopping and eating, particularly in France, gardening and collecting cookery books, both old and new.

The illustrator

Joanna Isles Freeman graduated from Glasgow School of Art with first class honours in Graphic Design. She worked as an illustrator for the BBC, notably on *Playschool*, and she devised and illustrated *A Proper Tea* (Collins and Brown). She has illustrated many children's books, including *The Twelve Days of Christmas*, *A Child's Garden of Verses* and *The Nutcracker* (Pavilion) and she is currently the designer of the commemorative china for the Royal Palaces. She lives in Oxfordshire with her two young daughters and her husband, broadcaster David Freeman.

CELEBRATIONS
RECIPES FOR FESTIVE OCCASIONS

SIMONE SEKERS

ILLUSTRATED BY
JOANNA ISLES FREEMAN

THE NATIONAL TRUST

This book is, as always, dedicated with thanks
to the encouragement and patient eating of my
husband David, our family and friends.

First published in Great Britain in 1995
by National Trust (Enterprises) Ltd
36 Queen Anne's Gate
London
SW1H 9AS

ISBN 0 7078 0183 4

British Library Cataloguing-in-Publication Data.
A catalogue record of this book is available from the British Library.

Designed by Newton Engert Partnership

Phototypeset in Monotype Photina 747
by Southern Positives and Negatives (SPAN), Lingfield, Surrey

Printed in Hong Kong
by South Sea International Press Ltd

Registered charity number 205846

CONTENTS

INTRODUCTION

Many of the greatest country houses in the ownership and care of the National Trust were themselves built as celebrations. Such houses are never likely to be cosy. Take the great Marble Hall at Clandon in Surrey, or at Kedleston in Derbyshire – it is difficult to feel anything but dwarfed by such magnificence. But fill either with people and the point of these rooms becomes clear. Celebrating in such houses is a fine experience, and one many of us can now enjoy at events held at Trust houses throughout the country.

All those who enjoy the annual carol concerts at Clandon know how wonderful the singing sounds amidst all that marble, but there are other ways of enjoying the surroundings. Every time we haul the picnic hamper, the table and chairs and rugs, the cool-bag full of chilled wine and beer and mineral water, out of the car and up and down slippery grass slopes to join in some jollity at Stowe or Stourhead, Claremont or Clumber, Fountains Abbey or Felbrigg Hall, we are just the latest in a long line. Carousing in the open air has been traditional in the wide open spaces which adjoin stately homes in Britain for several centuries. Once the countryside had been tamed sufficiently to make it comfortable to relax in, bucolic feasting began to emerge as a form of celebration, particularly when it meant entertaining thousands of tenants, staff and neighbours.

More intimate celebrations were conducted in the great dining rooms. At these smaller gatherings, mergers and unions were planned between one family and another, with or without the added complication of love. Dinners were held to engineer some political jerrymandering, to celebrate its success, or to entertain royalty. Some of the noblest families were granted their titles after a fine meal held in the splendour of a state dining room refurbished at enormous expense in their honour. In banqueting houses hidden in conveniently leafy groves or high up on roofs amongst chimney stacks, romantic liaisons were undoubtedly effected. It might even be said that much of the history of the National Trust itself was mapped out over meals and around tables as diverse as a millstone in Surrey and a scrubbed kitchen table in North Wales.

So this is a book to celebrate those celebrations, amatory, political, sporting, social, or financial, to celebrate the centenary of the greatest conservation organisation

in the world. I have looked at the way in which certain events were celebrated at properties owned by the Trust, and then made them relevant for today. Where records reveal what was eaten, I have translated menus and dishes into recipes cookable in our modern kitchens, taking into account the pressures upon our time.

It has been more difficult to find food which, today, we would regard as truly celebratory. Once upon a time, meat, so hard to come by in any quantity for most, was the epitome of feasting. Reading about the vast quantities of food organised for feasts such as those at Petworth (page 59), or Erddig (page 15), by far the largest element is meat, as well as poultry and game. As not all of us now regard meat in the same light, I have included vegetarian options. It is also now possible to find year-round versions of what used to be seasonal delicacies. I found it quite easy to buy asparagus in January to test recipes, but was really very relieved to find that it was impossible to get Seville oranges in June – some things are still sacred. Nonetheless I cheated since I had some in the freezer, another modern advantage we have over cooks of previous generations. So what used to constitute special treats, like the strawberries laboriously produced by a head gardener for a birthday in early spring, or hothouse peaches to grace an Edwardian sideboard at Christmas, have lost some of their glamour. And, because this book is about the National Trust, I have tried to keep to variations of national recipes, only venturing further afield where relevant. I have drawn on our own great cooks – Mrs Beeton, Hannah Glasse, Mrs Raffald *et al* – since they so clearly reflect the kind of food being eaten at the time.

How we eat, as well as what we eat, has also changed, but perhaps it is time to revive the old style of eating *à la française*, with numerous dishes for few courses, all set on the table at once. The Victorians turned from it when they embraced the newer fashion, *diner à la russe*, with a succession of courses, each one borne in by a servant who placed the dish on the sideboard, from which it was served. If this was somewhat less labour-intensive in the kitchen, since the cook had time to draw breath between each course instead of labouring to have everything ready at the same time, it was splendid affirmation, in the dining room, that you could afford the servants necessary to serve you at table.

Recently, after a symposium on provisioning the country house, I had the opportunity to try the old way. First, a great tureen of soup was brought in on its own, with which we were familiar. Then, when we had done justice to that, the table was laden with a roast, a fricassee, a piece of poached salmon, a savoury pudding,

several vegetable dishes, and numerous 'side dishes'. We needed some persuading by our host, a food historian, to take some of everything, a slice of the roast beef with some of the fricasseed chicken, and the pudding, the peas, the potatoes, the pickles, the poached salmon. Why we were so hesitant beats me, in retrospect, since we happily load our plates at a Chinese restaurant and think nothing of it. Then came the dessert course – compotes, syllabubs, a trifle and, something of a surprise at this stage of the meal, slices of roast duck breast as a savoury. This we did eat from a separate plate although the damson compote would have gone well with it. The dishes had all been cooked from recipes in an early nineteenth-century Yorkshire manuscript book, probably collected when this style of serving food was still usual.

On page 102 I have suggested a simpler version of a meal served *à la française*, with fewer dishes but all chosen so that they would be perfectly acceptable eaten alongside one another. It is an interesting experiment to try, perhaps to celebrate the refurbishment of an old house, or as an excuse for dressing in period. In fact, although the menus are arranged to celebrate events that might have occurred in the diary of a country house, they are meant simply to provide inspiration for any celebration, whether intimate or *en masse*. The vast quantities which were cooked to feed vast numbers are not reflected in the recipes in this book – all are in modest measurements. Our great advantage is that instead of temperamental servants, we have gadgets. These can be unreliable too, but food processors and blenders do not fall in love, leave in a huff, or cook the books. So any recipes, such as the quenelles on page 44 and the lobster cutlets on page 144, once requiring much pounding and sieving, can be made in minutes. They look impressive, sound daunting, taste delicious, and are amazingly easy.

As you plan a menu which might have wooed royalty, bribed a politician, or laid the foundation of a new dynasty, just imagine the dining room of your favourite National Trust property, or an elegant little Greek temple curtained by trees. It helps enormously with the chores.

ACKNOWLEDGEMENT

Very many thanks are due to the hard-pressed staff of the National Trust for all their help and kindness. But in the case of this particular book I would also like to thank the authors, past and present, of the informative, entertaining, and absorbing property handbooks. In the search for historical titbits I have read my way through every single one and have never enjoyed myself so much. And to the support team – Margaret Willes (the Publisher), Sheila Mortimer, Penny Clarke, Caroline Worlledge and Kate Crookenden – grateful thanks indeed.

HOW TO USE THIS BOOK

The suggested menus for the various celebrations are just that – suggestions. To make assembling the menu for your particular festivity easier, a subject index is divided into types of dish: Soups, First Courses, Meat, Game & Poultry Dishes and so on.

The number each menu will feed is given, the largest number being twenty-four. If this seems odd in a book about feasting, I have always found it easier, in my domestic-sized kitchen, to deal with a recipe for ten, say, doubling or trebling it as necessary, and even cooking it in batches and freezing each batch, than trying to imagine what size saucepan I would need to cook potatoes for thirty. And if you are asking others to help with a community celebration, cooking for ten is less daunting, so you will probably get more help!

In the introduction to each chapter I have given alternative suggestions to the specified menus. For instance, I have not given a menu for a christening tea, or a child's birthday tea, but have given ideas for how menus for either might be fashioned from items in other menus.

It is becoming increasingly obvious, as more and more of us have fan ovens and discover their eccentricities, that it is wise to reckon at least 10 minutes less cooking time and a reduction in temperature of about 10°C (20°F) from the cooking time and temperature of a conventional oven. This is particularly so in the case of cakes, especially fruit cakes.

Weights and measures are given in both metric and imperial. It is unwise to mix the two because the conversions are approximate. Where measurements are merely given in, for example, tablespoons, it is because the quantity is not crucial and you can adjust to suit your own, and your guests', tastes.

AMERICAN EQUIVALENTS

As the following conversions are approximate, it is essential to use all American, or all metric, or all imperial measures when following the recipes.

Crushed biscuits Dried breadcrumbs	1 US cup	=	2 oz	=	50 g
Peas Flaked almonds	1 US cup	=	4 oz	=	125 g
Flour Cornflour Dried fruit	1 US cup	=	5 oz	=	150 g
Fresh fruit Chopped peel	1 US cup	=	6 oz	=	175 g
Sugar Pearl barley	1 US cup	=	7 oz	=	200 g
Fats Cream cheese	1 US cup	=	8 oz	=	225 g
Apple purée Fruit pulp	1 US cup	=	9 oz	=	250 g
Liquids	1 US cup	=	8 fl oz	=	225 ml
	2 US cups (1 US pint)	=	16 fl oz	=	475 ml

CELEBRATING
INHERITANCE

CELEBRATING INHERITANCE

In the long history of old estates, the coming-of-age of the heir was an excuse for a series of celebratory feasts, for friends, neighbours, tenants and staff. The quantities of food consumed were vast, the logistics of planning such events considerable. Viscount Lumley's coming-of-age in 1878 required 25 sheep, 16 haunches venison, 165 game birds, 300 fowls, 336 quarts of milk, 560 cauliflowers, 100 pounds of grapes – and so on, to feed a daily total ranging from 226 to 1,248 over ten days.

Such revelry could get out of hand. When Lord Hartington inherited as 6th Duke of Devonshire in 1811, a huge feast was held for the tenantry at *Hardwick Hall*, in Derbyshire. An unsuspecting tourist, a Quaker called William Hewitt, had walked over from Mansfield on the fine May day to view the house. Instead of a scene of rural peace, he found plum puddings and joints of roast beef being hurled from the windows and ale cascading everywhere, in what must have seemed to his shocked eyes a truly bacchanalian orgy.

The coming-of-age in 1770 of Sir Watkin Williams-Wynn, neighbour and close friend of Philip Yorke of *Erddig*, Clwyd, required a huge 'shopping list' – 30 bullocks, of which one was roast whole, 50 hogs, 50 calves, 80 sheep, 18,000 eggs, 6,000 [heads of?] asparagus, 30 hogshead of ale and 120 dozen of wine. But then there were 15,000 people to be entertained at Wynnstay, Sir Watkin's house. Rather different was the quiet affair which ushered in Simon Yorke's inheritance of *Erddig* in 1924. The family fortunes were on the wane, and as Merlin Waterson notes in his book *The Servants' Hall*, the impressive photograph of family and staff taken on the steps was misleading, as many of the servants had been hired for the occasion, and were not part of the household.

Most records confirm that the food provided at these feasts was ample in quantity, but of a fairly simple nature; roast meat, pies and puddings. I have kept to this tradition in the menus that follow. And though our celebrations today most often take the form of dinner parties, I have not ignored larger feasts. Look on the next pages for a traditional menu for eight, a vegetarian menu for twelve and a summer menu for twelve.

A Coming-of-age Dinner

Chilled Consommé with Caviar and Savoury Biscuits
Roast Sirloin of Beef with Mushroom Sauce
Carrots in Madeira
Potato and Celeriac Purée
Rich Chocolate Cake with Ruby Oranges
Stilton with Celery, Comice Pears

for eight

Chilled Consommé with Caviar and Savoury Biscuits

2 tins condensed beef consommé
2 jars black lumpfish roe
1 carton crème fraîche
fresh celery leaves – see method

FOR THE SAVOURY BISCUITS

225g (8oz) plain flour
100g (4oz) butter
185g (6½oz) grated strongly
  flavoured cheese – Parmesan,
  Gruyère, mature Cheddar or
  a mixture
1 large egg
salt and black pepper
few drops Tabasco
cayenne

This is simplicity itself, though no-one would guess this from its taste or appearance. It is excellent accompanied by a celebratory champagne or dry sparkling wine.

Put the tins of consommé to chill in the fridge. Make up the cheese pastry for the savoury biscuits. Rub the butter into the flour, stir in the cheese and seasoning (use plenty of freshly ground black pepper and do not be too sparing with the salt, although if you use Parmesan allow for the fact that it is a salty cheese). Stir in the beaten egg and mix until the pastry comes together in a ball. Knead briefly and leave to rest in a cool place for an hour or so. Then roll out on a lightly floured board to about 1cm (¼in) thick and cut into finger-length straws about 2cm (½in) wide. Arrange on a greased baking sheet and bake for 10 minutes at 200°C/400°F/Gas 6, or until golden brown. Put on a rack to cool and dust with a little cayenne while still warm. You can make these in advance and freeze them, but heat them in the warm oven with the resting beef before serving with the consommé.

To assemble, empty the tins of consommé into a bowl and cut roughly with a knife. Put 1½ tablespoons into each of 8 ramekins; put a dessertspoon of crème fraîche on top, then

a teaspoon of lumpfish roe on the crème fraîche, and finally a few finely chopped celery leaves (use the nicely blanched ones from the middle of a head of celery). Keep cold until ready to eat, and serve with the warmed savoury biscuits.

Roast Sirloin of Beef with Mushroom Sauce

2kg (4–5lb) boned and rolled sirloin of beef
sprigs fresh thyme
salt and pepper
olive oil
stock and red wine for the gravy – see method

FOR THE SAUCE

275g (10oz) flat mushrooms
about 450ml (¾pt) beef stock – made either from the beef bones from the joint or a beef stock cube
50g (2oz) butter
50g (2oz) flour
sprig fresh thyme
1 clove garlic, crushed
salt and freshly ground black pepper
1 wineglass red wine – see method
2 tablespoons coarse grain mustard
1 dessertspoon crème fraîche

Preheat the oven to 225°C/450°F/Gas 8. Season the beef, rub it with olive oil and put it in a roasting tin with the thyme underneath the meat. Roast for 25 minutes per 500g (1lb), plus 25 minutes, for a medium rare finish.

Meanwhile, make the sauce. Dice the mushrooms fairly finely, stalks and all, and cook them gently in the red wine until tender. Tip into a sieve over a measuring jug to collect the juices. Melt the butter in a heavy pan, stir in the flour and return to a low heat to cook gently until a pale coffee colour. Add the strained mushroom juices to the beef stock to make up to 600ml (1pt) of liquid and add, off the heat, to the flour and butter mixture, stirring vigorously. Return to the heat and stir until the sauce comes to the boil and thickens. Add the thyme and the garlic and leave to cook on the lowest possible heat for about 20 minutes. Remove the thyme and garlic and add the mushrooms, stir well and remove from the heat; press cling film over the surface to stop a skin forming, and keep the sauce warm until the beef is ready. At about the time you take the beef from the oven, stir the mustard and crème fraîche into the sauce and taste for seasoning, then pour into a sauce boat.

When the beef is cooked place it on a warm serving dish and leave to rest in the switched off oven, with the door ajar. Pour off some of the fat. Then, using about 600ml (1pt) beef stock and red wine mixed together, make a gravy in the roasting pan, stirring in all the bits and pieces and simmering until it is reduced by about a third. Strain into another sauce boat.

17

Carrots in Madeira

900g (2lb) carrots, peeled and
cut lengthways into batons
25g (1oz) butter
salt and freshly ground pepper
2 tablespoons madeira
chopped parsley

Put the carrots in a wide, heavy pan with the butter, just enough water to cover, a pinch of salt and a grinding of pepper. Bring to the boil in the open pan and simmer fast until the water has evaporated and the carrots are tender. Add the madeira to the remaining buttery juices and stir gently so as not to break up the carrots. Simmer for a minute or so, dust with chopped parsley and serve.

Potato and Celeriac Purée

1kg (2¼lb) King Edward
potatoes
1 large celeriac
squeeze lemon juice
about 150ml (¼pt) warm milk
1 clove garlic (optional)
15g (½oz) butter
freshly grated nutmeg
salt and freshly ground black
pepper

Peel the potatoes, cut into large cubes and cook in boiling salted water with the clove of garlic, if you are using it. Peel and cube the celeriac and cook it in a separate pan of boiling salted water to which you have added a squeeze of lemon juice to stop the celeriac going grey. When both vegetables are tender, drain well, then mash them together with the milk and butter, seasoning with extra salt if necessary and with a little grated nutmeg. Add extra warm milk if necessary – the mixture should not be too stiff – and beat hard so that it is as light as possible.

Rich Chocolate Cake

For the cake, use the recipe
on page 131

FOR THE ICING

150g (5oz) good plain chocolate
25g (1oz) unsalted butter
1 tablespoon thick cream
pinch cinnamon
50g (2oz) white chocolate

To ice: place the plain chocolate in a bowl over a pan of hot water and, when it has melted, stir in the butter, cream and cinnamon. Pour over the cake and leave to set. Grate the white chocolate over the top, using the coarsest grater to produce curls, rather than crumbs.

Ruby Oranges

8 ruby or blood oranges
2 pomegranates
sugar to taste
few drops rose water

Peel the oranges thickly, removing all the pith, then slice them across as thinly as possible, removing any pips. Do this on a plate so that you catch the juice. Arrange in a shallow bowl, putting all the ragged slices underneath and reserving

the neatest for the top. Sprinkle with a little sugar – much will depend on the sweetness of the oranges. Cut the pomegranates in half, scoop out about 4 teaspoonfuls of the seeds and scatter on top of the oranges. Squeeze the juice from the pomegranate halves with an orange squeezer, then strain and mix with the rose water before pouring over the orange slices. The colour and the flavour of this is spectacular, but if ruby oranges are not available, you can use tangerines, clementines or navel oranges instead.

Stilton with Celery, Comice Pears

The pears to serve with the cheese should be buttery soft and melting – as they are never sold. It is best to buy them well in advance and put them in a bowl with other ripe fruit to aid their ripening. If you cannot get Doyenné du Comice pears, look for Williams Bon Chrétien. Choose Stilton which is cream coloured with a good network of blue veining. If you have to buy a piece which is incarcerated in plastic, release it so that it can breathe for at least two hours before eating.

Vegetarian Dinner Party

Root Vegetables in a Walnut Oil Dressing
Walnut Bread
Ragout of Wild Mushrooms
Two-rice Timbale
Broccoli with Roast Red Peppers
Walnut Ice-cream with Apricot Sauce
Vegetarian Cheeses with Cobnuts

for twelve

Root Vegetables in a Walnut Oil Dressing

450g (1lb) each carrots,
    celeriac, beetroot, salsify or
    scorzonera

FOR THE DRESSING

2 tablespoons sherry vinegar
6 tablespoons walnut oil
salt and freshly ground pepper
celery leaves

Peel the vegetables and cut the carrots and salsify or scorzonera into rings and the celeriac and beetroot into batons. Drop the celeriac and salsify or scorzonera into water to which you have added a generous squeeze of lemon juice to stop them discolouring. Steam the vegetables separately until just tender – do not undercook them or you will sacrifice their subtle flavours, but equally do not let them go soft. Arrange them on individual plates and drizzle over the dressing made by blending the sherry vinegar with the walnut oil, salt and pepper. Scatter chopped celery leaves over the top. Serve warm with warm walnut bread.

Walnut Bread

685g (1½lb) strong plain flour
15g (¾oz) fresh yeast, or
    1 sachet easy-blend dried
    yeast
1½ teaspoons salt
60g (2½oz) walnut pieces,
    toasted and cooled
2 tablespoons walnut oil
about 450ml (¾pt) lukewarm
    water

In a large mixing bowl, blend the salt, flour and walnuts and leave in a warm place for an hour or so. Then stir in the dried yeast, if using, and add the oil and almost all the water. Mix until you have a smooth dough which leaves the sides of the bowl clean. If you are using fresh yeast (and it does give a better flavour), blend this until smooth with a little of the warm water and add it at the same time as the rest of the water and oil. Knead the dough until it is lithe, springy and smooth, then form it into a ball, cut a cross right through and replace it in the mixing bowl. Wrap the bowl in a large plastic carrier bag and leave in a warm place until the dough has at least doubled in size, which will take a minimum of 2 hours, depending on the warmth of the resting place. You can also leave it to rise slowly overnight. Knead it again and shape it into a long sausage. Double the ends underneath and fit it into a non-stick loaf tin. Heat the oven to 225°C/450°F/Gas 8. Leave the bread to rise again until it appears over the rim of the tin, then bake for 40–45 minutes, lowering the heat to 180°C/360°F/Gas 4 after 20 minutes. Turn the loaf out and tap it on the base, it will sound hollow when it is ready. Cool on a rack, wrapped in a clean tea cloth if you prefer a soft crust. If you want to freeze it leave it at least 12 hours until quite cold, before wrapping very well and freezing.

Ragout of Wild Mushrooms

350g (12oz) each shitake,
    oyster and chestnut
    mushrooms
50g (2oz) each dried ceps
    and chanterelles or
225g (8oz) flat mushrooms
225g (8oz) finely sliced mild
    Spanish onion
3 cloves garlic, chopped
900ml (1½pt) water or
    vegetable stock
3 tablespoons olive oil
4 generous tablespoons crème
    fraîche
salt and crushed allspice

This is a rich, intensely-flavoured dish which calls for the sort of 'wild' mushrooms now found in most supermarkets – oyster, shitake, chestnut. I also like to add dried ceps and chanterelles for their particular depth of flavour; their extra advantage is that the water in which they soak makes a good alternative to the vegetable stock suggested in the recipe.

If using dried ceps and chanterelles bring the water to the boil and pour it over them, then leave to soak for about 35 minutes. Slice the other mushrooms, wiping off any grit with a damp cloth. Soften the onion in the oil for about 10 minutes, then add the mushrooms (both fresh and dried) and garlic and cook gently, with a lid on the pan, for about 20 minutes or until the juices have begun to run. Add the vegetable stock, or the strained soaking water from the dried mushrooms, and continue to simmer gently until all the mushrooms are tender. Season with salt and allspice. Remove from the heat and keep warm. Just before serving, stir in the crème fraîche.

Two-rice Timbale

450g (1lb) arborio risotto rice
175g (6oz) wild rice
5 shallots, finely chopped
about 1·2l (2pt) hot vegetable
    stock
4 tablespoons olive oil
2 bay leaves
large sprig thyme
salt and pepper
4 tablespoons finely grated
    Parmesan cheese
finely chopped parsley

Cook the wild rice in lightly salted simmering water for 20 minutes, then drain well. Soften the shallots in the olive oil for 5 minutes, then stir in the wild and the arborio rice (if you cannot get this special Italian risotto rice use ordinary long grain, but rinse it very well before you add it to the shallots), mixing well until every grain is covered with hot oil. Add the herbs and just enough of the hot stock to cover the rice and cook gently, uncovered, until the stock is absorbed. Continue to add the stock, a ladleful at a time, until the rice is tender and the liquid absorbed. This will take about 25 minutes. Check for seasoning. Off the heat, stir in the Parmesan and put the risotto into an oiled cake tin or ring mould, cover with a piece of foil and keep warm.

To serve, remove the foil and invert the cake tin or ring mould on a warmed serving dish and unmould. Spoon as

much of the mushroom ragout around or into the centre as you can and serve the rest separately. Sprinkle with freshly chopped parsley.

Broccoli with Roast Red Peppers

900g (2lb) broccoli
4 red peppers

Halve the peppers and arrange them, cut side down, on an oiled baking sheet. Roast them in a hot oven (225°C/450°F/ Gas 8) for about 25 minutes until the skin is blackened and blistered and the peppers are soft. Take them from the oven and cover them with a damp tea cloth until they are cool enough to handle. Peel off the blistered skin, then cut the peppers into thin strips. This can be done some time in advance. Steam the broccoli, broken into florets, and when just tender add the strips of pepper to the steamer to reheat. Place broccoli and peppers on a warmed dish, sprinkle with a little sea salt and serve with the mushrooms and rice timbale.

Walnut Ice-cream with Apricot Sauce

175g (6oz) walnut pieces
150g (5oz) soft brown sugar
450ml (¾pt) whipping cream
450ml (¾pt) double cream

FOR THE SAUCE

400g (14oz) can apricots
    in fruit juice
3–4 tablespoons apricot jam
grated rind of half a lemon
squeeze lemon juice
2 tablespoons apricot brandy
    or amaretto liqueur
amaretti or ratafias

To make the ice-cream, toast the walnut pieces under the grill, leave to cool then chop coarsely. Whip the creams together until thick and billowy but not stiff, then fold in the walnuts and the sugar (having made sure there are no lumps). Pour into a shallow plastic box, cover and freeze. After about 2 hours stir the ice-cream well. Return to the freezer for another 10 hours or so, stirring once or twice more.

To make the sauce, heat the apricots in their juice with the jam and the lemon rind over a gentle heat, then purée until reasonably smooth in a food processor or blender. Return to the pan and heat again, this time adding lemon juice until you get a good balance between sweet and sharp. Add the chosen liqueur. Serve hot or cold.

To serve, spoon a pool of sauce on each plate and arrange two scoops of the walnut ice-cream on top. Garnish with amaretti or ratafias.

Vegetarian Cheeses with Cobnuts

Many good cheeses are now made with vegetarian rennet. If you have a helpful delicatessen or cheese shop discuss the matter with them. Kentish cobnuts are in season early in the autumn and are delicious, fresh and milky and quite unlike the dried-out hazelnuts we get at Christmas. If they are unavailable, serve walnuts instead, also best in early autumn.

Summer Lunch Party

Chilled Lettuce Soup
Salmon Baked with Fennel
Fennel Butter Sauce
Festive Summer Salad
Raspberries in a Bowl of Rose Ice-cream
Peaches in Sparkling Elderflower Syrup
Selection of Soft Cheeses

for twelve

Chilled Lettuce Soup

2 large cos lettuces, washed and shredded
3 bunches spring onions, finely sliced
2·5l (4pt) hot vegetable stock
50g (2oz) butter
2 tablespoons flour
1 carton crème fraîche
salt and pepper
finely chopped tarragon

If the weather turns cold this soup can be served hot. It is best made with vegetable stock so that it can be enjoyed by all your guests.

Melt the butter in a large heavy pan and add the spring onions and a sprinkling of salt. Leave to soften over a low heat for about 5 minutes. Add the shredded lettuce, mix well with the spring onions and then add the stock. Simmer gently for 20–25 minutes, until the ribs of the lettuce leaves are tender. Cool a little then blend, process or sieve. Return to a clean pan. Mix the flour to a smooth paste with some of the crème fraîche and add this gradually to the soup, whisking as you do so and with the soup on a low heat. Bring up to

the boil, then remove and add the rest of the crème fraîche. Leave to get cold, then check the seasoning. Chill for 2 hours before serving, and sprinkle with chopped tarragon.

Salmon Baked with Fennel

2–2·5kg (4–5lb) whole
  salmon, gutted
50g (2oz) butter
large bunch fennel leaves
salt and freshly ground pepper
8 tablespoons medium dry
  white wine

Heat the oven to 150°C/300°F/Gas 2. Melt the butter and brush it over a large sheet of foil which will hold the salmon comfortably. Chop the fennel, put some in the fish and the rest on the foil, placing the seasoned salmon on top and adding any remaining butter, and the wine. Fold the foil around the fish, making sure the edges are well sealed together. Place the fish parcel directly on the bars of the oven shelf and cook for 1¼ hours. Take carefully from the oven and open the parcel. Lift the skin gently away from the flesh on one side and slide the fish on to a warmed serving dish, skinned side up. Strain the cooking juices over it and garnish with more fennel leaves.

Fennel Butter Sauce

1 small onion, finely chopped
8 tablespoons dry white wine
8 tablespoons tarragon vinegar
450g (1lb) butter
3 tablespoons finely chopped
  fennel

This is a thick butter sauce, lighter than a hollandaise and easier to make, but it cannot be made much in advance.

Cube the butter and chill it in the fridge until very hard. Put the onion, white wine and vinegar into a small heavy pan and simmer steadily until the onion is soft and the liquid reduced by half. Set aside until ready to make the sauce. Transfer this mixture to a basin over a pan of hot, but not boiling, water. Add two or three cubes of butter to the bowl and whisk so that it melts to a cream but does not become oily. Continue to add the butter, whisking all the time and checking that it does not get too hot. When all the butter has been used up and the sauce is a pale creamy colour, stir in the chopped fennel and serve. To prevent everything being done at the last minute, you can stand the sauce over *warm* water for about 30 minutes.

The fish and its sauce are best served simply, with green beans and Jersey Royal potatoes.

Festive Summer Salad

Make up a combination of every sort of salad leaf you can find and decorate with edible flowers such as nasturtium, marigold, borage, small pansies, chives, rose petals. Sprinkle with chopped fresh herbs – chervil, chives, tarragon, basil. At the very last minute mix the dressing by combining tarragon vinegar with a light olive oil in the proportion of one of vinegar to six of oil. Season with salt, freshly ground white pepper and a pinch of sugar and add to the salad.

Raspberries in a Bowl of Rose Ice-cream

3 egg whites
200g (7oz) sugar
juice of ½ orange
150ml (¼pt) water
2 dessertspoons rose water
2 drops red food colouring
450ml (¾pt) whipping cream
1kg (2lb) raspberries
caster sugar
roses or rose petals

Combine the sugar, orange juice and water in a small pan, put over a low heat to dissolve the sugar. Meanwhile, whip the egg whites until stiff. When the sugar has dissolved raise the heat and boil the syrup hard for 3 minutes. Pour it in a steady stream on to the egg whites while continuing to beat hard, then carry on beating until you have a thick and billowy meringue-like mixture. Add the rose water and food colouring. Whip the cream until softly thick and fold in to the meringue, making sure it is well blended. Place the ice-cream in a decorative, preferably glass, bowl and then place another, smaller bowl in the centre. (It is now possible to buy a kit to make ice bowls.) Put the whole thing in the freezer. When ready to serve, remove the smaller bowl (pour a little warm water into it and leave it for a few seconds until you can lift it out) and fill the hollow with fresh raspberries, lightly dusted with caster sugar and decorated with fresh roses or rose petals.

Peaches in Sparkling Elderflower Syrup

12 ripe peaches
85ml (3 fl oz) elderflower
* cordial*
100g (4oz) sugar
300ml (½pt) water
150ml (¼pt) sparkling mineral
* water*

The elderflower cordial, widely available now in good food shops, gives a delicate flowery flavour to the sparkling syrup for this fruit salad.

Dissolve the sugar in the water, bring to the boil and boil hard for 3 minutes, add the elderflower cordial and leave to cool. Meanwhile, skin the peaches by dipping each in boiling water for a count of six, then slipping off the skin. Slice them into a bowl and pour over the syrup. Chill. About 30 minutes before serving add the sparkling mineral water to the peaches and syrup. Mix gently together. Decorate, if possible, with fresh elderflowers.

Selection of Soft Cheeses

The cheeses should, ideally, be those fresh milk cheeses of summer, creamy and mild. If you live in a good cheese-making area, such as Devon, you might be able to achieve this. If not, serve a soft garlic-and-herb cheese, a mild goats' cheese, a cream cheese to which you have added finely chopped dried tomatoes-in-oil, or some diced green olives, and a Caboc (a rich cream cheese from Scotland, rolled in toasted oatmeal).

POLITICAL
TRIUMPHS

POLITICAL TRIUMPHS

Political triumphs – and failures – are part of the history of many houses now owned by the National Trust. In certain families, like the Onslows of *Clandon*, in Surrey, who can boast three Speakers of the House of Commons, several generations followed political careers. At *Shugborough*, in Staffordshire, Thomas Anson was elected MP for Lichfield in 1747 by a cliff-hanging handful of votes, ousting the sitting Tory member and thus enabling future Ansons to become sitting members in their turn. William Willoughby Cole, of *Florence Court*, County Fermanagh, became MP for Enniskillen in 1761, following his father's footsteps. Later created Viscount Enniskillen, he subsequently graduated to an earldom. His son, the 2nd Earl, became MP for the area in his turn. *Newtown Town Hall* on the Isle of Wight, one of the Trust's most charming and peaceful properties, was once the scene of rowdy political debates as this tiny borough regularly returned two MPs to Parliament until 1835. Such scenes are hard to imagine now as the grass grows around it and the seabirds call overhead.

Other 'political' properties owned by the National Trust are *Cliveden*, *Chartwell* and *Hughenden*, Benjamin Disraeli's home until his death on 19 April 1881. Subsequently, this day became known as Primrose Day after Disraeli's favourite flower.

Little is known about the form political celebrations took. Sir Thomas Acland's Tory triumph in 1812 was celebrated by a dinner at *Killerton*, Devon, and Lady Onslow's Dinner Book lists the menus of political dinners held both at Clandon and their London house in Richmond Terrace, off Whitehall.

The following menus are not of any particular political complexion – they could equally well celebrate an election to a board of directors, of school governors, or a debating society. The first is based on the menus which appear in Lady Onslow's Dinner Book. She combined the popular dishes of the day to entertain those who were, perhaps, too busy discussing the issues to notice that they were eating a fairly humdrum series of dishes. Such a menu might seem elaborate now, but it is a typical Victorian formal dinner.

The menu for 12 May 1887, was:

Potage à la Julienne Royale
Truite Froide Flamande
Foies de Volaille en Brochette
Cotelettes d'Agneau à la Provençale
Haunche de Venison, Selle de Mouton
Canetons au cressons, Asperges en branches
Oeufs des Pluviers en Aspic
Tartes des Pêches Vertes
Eclairs aux Parmesan

I have used this as the inspiration for two menus, summer and winter. The season for plovers' eggs being now permanently closed, quails' eggs are a more than adequate equivalent. As for the green peach tarts – were these really made of furry green unripe peaches? I have substituted a fresh peach tart glazed with greengage jam and scattered with chopped pistachio nuts for the summer menu, and an apple tart glazed with peach jam and decorated with angelica 'leaves' for autumn or winter. The main ingredient of the Potage is not indicated, but the Julienne Royale was presumably the usual 'royal' garnish, a very solid egg custard cut into match-sticks when cold and added to the soup just before serving. This garnish did little to affect the overall flavour of the soup and was just another way – there were so many – of showing that you could afford a chef and that he in turn could employ a minion to cut shapes out of cold egg custard. Croûtons are quicker and nicer.

A Victorian Political Dinner

Chestnut Soup with Bacon Croûtons
Saddle or Haunch of Venison with Plum and Rosemary Sauce
Gratin of Potatoes
Tarte aux Pommes Vertes

Winter – for eight

Chestnut Soup with Bacon Croûtons

450g (1lb) peeled chestnuts
  (either fresh, vacuum packed
  or dried and soaked)
3 medium potatoes
2 sticks celery, finely chopped
2·5 l (3½pt) stock (see method)
1 bayleaf
salt and pinch allspice
cream to finish

FOR THE BACON CROÛTONS

3 slices stale brown bread, cubed
4 rashers unsmoked middle-
  back bacon, diced
3 tablespoons groundnut oil

Game, or a not-too-salty ham, stock are both ideal for this soup, but you can use a beef stock cube instead.

Peel and cube the potatoes, then add them to the stock with the chestnuts, celery and bayleaf and simmer all together for about 30 minutes, until the vegetables are soft. Blend or process until smooth, then season to taste with salt and ground allspice. If the soup is too thick, thin it with a little hot milk or some more stock.

Make the bacon croûtons by frying the bread and the bacon until really crisp in the hot groundnut oil. If you are fortunate enough to have good dry-cured bacon it might yield enough of its own fat to make the oil unnecessary. Drain on kitchen paper and keep warm in the oven with the door ajar (or they will go soft). Add a swirl of cream to each bowl of soup as you serve and hand the bacon croûtons separately.

Saddle or Haunch of Venison with Plum and Rosemary Sauce

1 saddle or haunch venison
about 225g (8oz) streaky
  unsmoked bacon
2 teaspoons juniper berries,
  crushed
few sprigs rosemary
salt and pepper
olive oil

FOR THE SAUCE

jar good quality plum jam
generous sprig rosemary
2 wineglasses red wine
2 cloves

Venison is a lean, close-textured meat which needs plenty of lubrication as it cooks. Saddles are more easily available than haunches, but the latter are worth seeking out.

Preheat the oven to 170°C/350°F/Gas 4. Rub the meat with olive oil, season well with salt and pepper and crushed juniper berries, then cover the surface with the bacon rashers. Put in a roasting tin on the sprigs of rosemary (if you cannot get the fresh herb, dried will do just as well) and put to roast for 20 minutes per 500g (1lb), plus 20 minutes. Baste it every half-hour with the pan juices.

Make the plum sauce while the venison cooks. Put all the ingredients into a small, heavy pan and cook gently until the jam has melted, then set aside, with a lid on the pan. Remove the bacon 45 minutes before the venison has finished cooking, spoon some of the sauce over the joint to form a glaze, and then return to the oven to finish cooking. Remove the

rosemary and cloves from the rest of the sauce and sieve so that it is fairly smooth. Keep warm.

When the venison is cooked, put it on a warmed serving dish and leave to rest in the switched-off oven, with the door ajar. Make the gravy from the pan juices and sediments plus two generous glasses of wine and one of water. Boil well to reduce and then strain into a gravy boat.

Gratin of Potatoes

This is an anglicised version of gratin dauphinois; it is less rich, but no less good. Parboil some potatoes in their skins, then peel and slice thickly. Arrange in a gratin dish, pour over just enough hot milk to come level with the top and push some rosemary down among the potato slices. Season well, dot with butter and bake on a shelf below the venison for about an hour.

Tarte aux Pommes Vertes

225g (8oz) plain flour
100g (4oz) unsalted butter
2 dessertspoons icing sugar
pinch salt
1 large egg, beaten

FOR THE FILLING

10–12 Cox's apples, cored
  and thinly sliced
juice 1 lemon
50g (2oz) unsalted butter,
  melted
350g (12oz) jar peach jam
angelica

First, make the flan case. Sift together the flour, icing sugar and salt, then rub in the butter until the mixture is bread-crumb-like. Stir in the egg, mix to a dough, then knead briefly before wrapping and leaving in the fridge for about 30 minutes. Roll out on a floured board and use to line a 25cm (10in) flan tin with a removable base. Prick the base and line with non-stick baking parchment, then weigh down with pastry beans (dried beans will do, but ceramic pastry beans are best). Heat the oven to 220°C/425°F/Gas 7 and while it does put in a baking sheet to heat up as well. Place the pastry-lined flan tin on the sheet and bake for 10 minutes. Remove the paper and beans and lower the oven temperature to 175°C/350°F/Gas 4 and bake for another 8–10 minutes, until set.

Melt a couple of tablespoonfuls of the jam and brush it over the base of the flan case. Then toss the apple slices in the lemon juice and arrange them in concentric circles to cover the base neatly and attractively. Brush carefully with the melted butter, then bake at 175°C/350°F/Gas 4 for 25

minutes or until the apples are tender. Take the tart from the oven and allow to cool, then varnish thickly with the remaining jam, melted and sieved. Flatten out the angelica and cut simple leaves, arranging them in a pattern over the tart. Serve with slightly sweetened whipped cream, flavoured, if you like, with a pinch of cinnamon.

A Victorian Political Dinner

Smoked Trout with Asparagus
Pot-roast Guinea Fowl with Watercress, Foies des Volailles en Brochettes
Tartes aux Pêches Vertes

Summer – for four

Smoked Trout with Asparagus

4 fillets smoked trout
450g (1lb) asparagus
175g (6oz) fromage frais
4 tablespoons crème fraîche
salt and Tabasco
squeeze of lemon juice

Snap off the tough ends of the asparagus stems and keep for soup, then cut off the tips plus about 4cm ($1\frac{1}{2}$in) stem. Cook the remaining sections of stem in boiling salted water, with the tip ends steaming above them in a steamer. Set the tip ends aside, drain the middle sections and purée them in a blender or processor, then cool. Mix the fromage frais with the crème fraîche, then add the purée, bit by bit, tasting as you go, until the mixture is well flavoured with asparagus. Season with salt and one or two drops of Tabasco, plus a squeeze of lemon juice if the mixture needs sharpening. Arrange the smoked trout and asparagus tips on each plate and then add a generous helping of the sauce. Serve with brown bread and butter.

Pot-roast Guinea Fowl with Watercress, Foies des Volailles en Brochettes

2 small or 1 large guinea fowl
2 tablespoons green peppercorns
    in brine, rinsed
generous bunch watercress
2 generous glasses dry white
    wine
4 tablespoons crème fraîche
225g (8oz) chicken livers
2 tablespoons balsamic vinegar
groundnut oil
salt and pepper

Guinea fowl is a domesticated game bird. Its flesh is similar to that of chicken, but has a slightly gamier flavour and is rather drier, which is why I suggest pot-roasting it. If you can find ones with giblets, so much the better, as you can include the livers among the chicken livers and the giblets will make a stock for the gravy.

Preheat the oven to 175°C/350°F/Gas 4. Season the guinea fowl(s) inside and out with salt and brown them well all over in the oil. Remove the stalks from the watercress and arrange them as a bed for the bird(s), in a casserole which fits them comfortably. Crush the drained peppercorns a little and add them together with the wine. Put on the lid of the casserole and cook for about an hour.

Meanwhile, sort out the livers, removing any greenish or yellowish bits which show signs of having been tainted by the bitter gall bladder, and thread them on to 4 fine metal skewers. Season with salt and pepper, dribble a little oil over them and grill for about 10 minutes under a hot grill, turning once. Keep warm. Chop the watercress leaves. When the guinea fowl(s) are tender (allow another 15 minutes or so if the casserole is earthenware), carve them into neat serving pieces and arrange on a warm plate. Tip the cooking juices and the juice from the carving process into a saucepan, discarding the watercress stalks. Add another glass of wine and bubble all together for about 5 minutes. Add the crème fraîche, then the finely chopped watercress leaves. Check the seasoning and pour over the guinea fowl(s). Arrange the brochettes on top, plus a tuft or two of watercress. Serve with new potatoes and green beans.

Tartes aux Pêches Vertes

*1 quantity of pastry as on
   page 32*

FOR THE FILLING

*4 large peaches
225g (8oz) greengage jam,
   warmed and sieved
85g (3oz) finely chopped
   pistachio nuts*

Roll out the pastry and cut into 4 circles about 9·5cm (3½in) in diameter. Arrange on a baking sheet and bake until pale golden brown at 175°C/350°F/Gas 4 for about 15 minutes. Cool on a wire rack, then brush each with the sieved greengage jam. Skin the peaches by dipping each one briefly in boiling water – the skins will slip off easily. Slice round the stones into neat slices and arrange in concentric circles on the pastry discs. Brush with more greengage jam and sprinkle lightly with the chopped nuts. These should not be assembled more than 2 hours before eating. Serve with whipped cream.

A Disraeli Dinner

**Eggs in Nests
Spring Lamb en Papillote with Baby Vegetables
'Primrose' Salad
Chancellor's Puddings (Hot or Iced)**

for four

Perhaps a Disraeli menu might be in order, simply to include what Mrs Hilda Leyel in her book, *Green Salads and Fruit Salads*, claimed to have been Disraeli's favourite salad. As this book was published in the 1930s, I feel the claim was posthumous. This is a springtime menu, and you can, of course, only use primroses if you have them growing in the garden. However, there are plenty of modern hybrids in other party political colours.

Eggs in Nests

1 dozen quails' eggs, or
*   4 hens' eggs*
4 long, slim leeks
300ml (½pt) lightly whipped
*   cream and fromage frais,*
*   mixed*
juice ½ lemon
4 tablespoons grapeseed
*   or sunflower oil*
salt and pepper
about 2 teaspoons chopped
*   chives*

Quails' eggs are ideal for this recipe, which marries the last of the leeks with the first of the chives in a light dressing, although the Victorians might well have thought it a little insubstantial.

Wash and trim the leeks, then slice across into rings about 1cm (½in) wide. Salt lightly then steam until tender. As they steam, make up the dressing with half the chives, lemon juice, oil, salt and pepper and as soon as the leeks are ready, toss them gently in this vinaigrette. Arrange some in a circle on each plate. Cover the eggs with cold water, add a teaspoonful of salt and bring to the boil. Time for 2 minutes for the quails' eggs and 10 minutes for the hens'. At the end of the cooking time, put the pan under a cold running tap, then peel the eggs as soon as you can handle them; in this way you avoid that grey ring around the yolk. Set aside. Spoon a circle of cream and fromage frais on the leeks, leaving a good margin of pale green leeks. Halve the quails' eggs, or quarter the hens', arrange them on the cream and scatter with the remaining chives.

Spring Lamb en Papillotte with Baby Vegetables

8 noisettes of spring lamb
12 baby carrots
8 small new potatoes – Jersey
*   Royals if possible*
8 tiny turnips
15g (1oz) butter
1 dessertspoon sunflower oil
generous sprig rosemary
salt and pepper

As English spring lamb is so very expensive, it is helpful to make its delicate flavour go a little further by cooking it with other things, in this case baby carrots and turnips and new potatoes.

Peel and boil the vegetables in salted water for 2 minutes, drain well. Heat the oven to 175°C/350°F/Gas 4. Cut 4 generous rectangles of baking parchment. Season the noisettes. Melt the butter and oil in a heavy pan, together with the rosemary, and leave over a low heat for a few minutes to infuse the fats with the rosemary flavour. Remove the herb, raise the heat a little and seal the noisettes briefly on both sides. Arrange a bed of vegetables on one half of each rectangle of paper and put a pair of noisettes on top. Fold the

paper over, pinching the edges tightly together. Put on a baking tray and cook for 25 minutes. Serve with green beans, and follow with the salad.

'Primrose' Salad

FOR THE SALAD

lambs' lettuce leaves
Little Gem lettuce leaves
chicory leaves
inside leaves from a head of
* celery*
a few primrose flowers and
* leaves*

FOR THE VINAIGRETTE

few strands of saffron, or a pinch
* of saffron powder*
1 teaspoon hot water
1 dessertspoon cider vinegar
6 dessertspoons light olive oil
salt and freshly ground white
* pepper*
finely chopped chervil

Whether Mrs Leyel's claim that this was Disraeli's favourite salad came from an entirely reliable source is not known, although the primrose was certainly his favourite flower. She also mentions a German salad combining primroses and cowslips. Unless you grow both in the garden, making this salad is out of the question. For today's 'Primrose Salad' I suggest adding a few home-grown flowers and leaves to a fresh green salad.

Toss the lamb's lettuce, lettuce, chicory and celery leaves together. Decorate with primrose flowers and leaves. To make the dressing, soak the saffron for a minute or two in the hot water, then add both water and saffron to the other ingredients and combine. Pour over the salad and mix at the last minute.

Chancellor's Puddings (Hot or Iced)

4 trifle sponges
4 eggs
450ml ($\frac{3}{4}$pt) rich Channel
* Island milk, or milk and*
* single cream mixed*
grated rind $\frac{1}{2}$ lemon
6 amaretti, crumbled, or
* 12 ratafias*
85g (3oz) glacé cherries,
* chopped*
85g (3oz) vanilla sugar
wineglass sherry – see method
10g ($\frac{1}{2}$oz) unsalted butter,
* melted – see method*

This very popular pudding, also known as Cabinet Pudding, appeared in almost every Victorian and Edwardian cookery book. In its most debased form – as a sort of bread-and-butter pudding popular with stingy landladies – it became the curse of boarding-house dinner tables. But it can, and should, be rich and delicious and deserves a revival, especially when served either hot, or iced, shaped in individual moulds.

HOT VERSION. Grease 4 individual pudding moulds or porcelain ramekins with the melted butter, then place a circle of baking parchment in the bottom of each. Beat the yolks of 2 eggs and the remaining 2 whole eggs, plus the sugar and lemon rind, in a basin. Bring the milk, or milk/cream mixture, to the boil and then pour on the eggs and sugar in a thin

stream, beating well. Cool a little while you crumble the sponge cakes and the amaretti into a basin, add the chopped cherries and mix well, then pour on the custard and stir thoroughly. Spoon some of the pudding mixture into each mould to come within 1 cm ($\frac{1}{2}$in) of the top, cover with more baking parchment and place the moulds in a saucepan containing enough simmering water to come halfway up the sides. Place a plate on top of the ramekins and then the lid on the saucepan, and steam gently for about 30 minutes, or until firm. Turn out on to individual plates and serve with the Apricot Sauce on page 22, which should be heated and then enlivened with the sherry.

COLD VERSION. Rinse the ramekins or pudding moulds with cold water, then line with cling film, pressing it down well all over the inside. Follow the directions above, but return the custard mixture to the pan and cook it gently, over the lowest possible heat, until it thickens to coat the back of the spoon. Then mix with the other ingredients and spoon into the moulds. Cool, then freeze. Place in the fridge about 30 minutes before serving, then turn out on to a pool of the Apricot Sauce. Garnish with spring flowers, and serve with whipped cream if you like.

SPORTING
ACHIEVEMENTS

SPORTING ACHIEVEMENTS

Of all sporting occasions at country houses, it is almost always the shooting lunch that springs to mind. For anyone who has been standing around in the heather, appetite sharpened by cold and, it must be admitted, boredom, those elegantly fitted lunch baskets full of warming food and cheering drink are an all-important focus to the day.

Shooting lunches are an obvious excuse for eating lots of warming, filling food on the grounds that you are likely to have burnt up ample calories during the morning's activities. But why restrict them to shooting events? For those who like to take their winter exercise less blood-thirstily, how about a walking lunch, a football lunch, or a tobogganing lunch? Those who prefer to stay at home in a warm kitchen can prearrange a meeting place and transport the food for the starving sportsmen. We are poor in this country at catering publicly for such events, with the notable exception of *Leith Hill Tower* high on the North Downs in Surrey. There, brave and generous-spirited souls fuel walkers and cyclists with ample mugs of home-made soup, nourishing sandwiches and thick slices of fruit cake, particularly appreciated on snowy days in midwinter. To avoid pubs which are grudging about offering anything sustaining to eat after 2pm, I suggest a menu that is transportable, if not exactly picnic food.

There are, of course, many other sporting events where the food is equally important. In the 1930s Mrs Ronnie Greville, socially aspiring hostess at *Polesden Lacey* in Surrey, entertained the Aga Khan regularly for Ascot. Her food was famous, simple (by the standards of the day) and perfect, although she was criticised for being unimaginative in what she offered to whom. To the Aga Khan, caviare and blinis, to the local vicar, Brown Windsor soup. Wouldn't the Aga Khan, mused her critic, have been intrigued by the soup, and the vicar uplifted by the caviare? Working through her Dinner Book, I have chosen a menu which is easy to emulate, and is fairly imaginative, although safe enough to offer anyone, Aga Khan or vicar.

Ballooning seems to be enjoying a revival. It is a pastime admirably suited to the English landscape, and it is often a bonus, on a balmy summer's afternoon, to see elegantly striped balloons floating over a Capability Brown park and its grazing deer. Taking note of the intrepid flight made by William Windham, of *Felbrigg*, Norfolk, in 1784, I have devised a meal for those with an adventurous spirit. This can be eaten at any time of day, since I understand that appetite must wait on a suitable prevailing wind.

Cricket, too, is a country house, as well as a village green, pursuit. Edward Hussey, of *Scotney Castle* in Kent, was a fine and enthusiastic cricketer and played for Kent *v.* Surrey in 1773, and for England against Surrey in 1797. He also helped to revive interest in what was to become another country-house sport, archery. In the eighteenth century both the ritual of afternoon tea and the game of cricket were in their infancy and the two had not been inextricably wedded together as they were to be later, the post-match tea becoming almost as important as the match itself. As Scotney also has an ice-house, ices might well have formed part of a tea party after the cricket match.

Mrs Greville's Ascot Dinner

Consommé Princesse
Salmon Quenelles with Sorrel Sauce
Salade de Saison
Strawberry Meringue Cream
Strawberries Romanof

for ten

Consommé Princesse

2 free-range chickens, each
   weighing about 1·75kg/ 3½lb
225g (8oz) shin beef
2 medium onions
4 large carrots
2 sticks of celery
large bunch herbs – parsley,
   thyme, bayleaf
3 cloves garlic
strip of lemon peel
2 cloves
1½ tablespoons coarse sea salt
1 teaspoon black peppercorns
350g (12oz) thin asparagus
3 tablespoons finely chopped
   chervil

This is a clear chicken soup, garnished in this labour-saving version with asparagus tips and chopped chervil. Such a consommé at Mrs Greville's dinners would have been further elaborated with a thickening of tapioca and the addition of tiny chicken dumplings. It is worth making your own consommé, as it will provide some very good cold chicken for the next day's picnic lunch – at Ascot, of course.

Split the chickens down the centre (or ask the butcher to do it), and put them in a large pan together with any giblets, except the livers. Add the beef, chopped into large cubes, the peeled carrots, split lengthways, the unpeeled onions each stuck with a clove, the garlic, and the herbs and strip of lemon peel tied in a neat bundle between the celery sticks. Add peppercorns – but not the salt – and 3 litres (5 pints) cold water. Bring slowly to the boil, then skim off the grey froth that appears on the surface. Lower the heat until you have a steady, gentle simmer and then add half the salt, cover the pan and leave cooking at that rate for 1¼ hours or until the chickens are cooked (I prefer to do this in the oven set at 150°C/300°F/Gas 2). Lift out the chickens and continue to simmer the stock, with the lid off the pan, for another 30 minutes to reduce it and concentrate the flavour. You should end up with about 2 litres (3 pints). Strain the stock (set aside the shin beef to make potted beef – see the recipe for Potted Meat on page 50) and check the seasoning, adding the rest of the salt if necessary, then leave to cool. To clarify it in the traditional manner, put the whites of two eggs, together with their crushed shells, into a pan and beat lightly, just enough to liquify the egg whites. Pour on the stock – it need not be absolutely cold – and bring slowly to the boil. As the consommé heats, the egg whites and shell will coagulate on the surface, drawing up all the debris in the stock, to form a sort of concrete-coloured pebble-dash on the surface. Simmer gently for 15 minutes to let the clarification take place, then draw aside. Line a sieve with muslin, or a new J-cloth, wrung out in hot water and pour the stock slowly through into a scrupulously clean bowl. If you prefer

to by-pass this lengthy but very satisfying process, simply strain the stock again after its final seasoning.

To serve, steam the asparagus until tender and cut the top 5–8cms (2–3ins) into little pieces, leaving the tips identifiable. Add a tablespoon of asparagus and a sprinkling of chervil to each serving of the consommé. For a more substantial soup, add some diced breast meat from the chickens, too.

Salmon Quenelles with Sorrel Sauce

685g (1½lb) fresh salmon, free of skin and bones
275g (10oz) fresh white breadcrumbs
275g (10oz) slightly salted butter, French or Dutch
300ml (½pt) milk
3 egg yolks
1 whole egg
salt, pepper, nutmeg
150ml (¼pt) white wine
1l (1¾pt) fish stock (use 2 fish stock cubes)
extra breadcrumbs

SORREL SAUCE

500ml (1pt) hot fish stock
50g (2oz) butter
50g (2oz) flour
75g (3oz) fresh sorrel
4 tablespoons crème fraîche or 150ml (¼pt) single cream
salt, pepper, nutmeg
breadcrumbs

These light fish dumplings come in many guises, by far the least interesting are those which are merely composed of egg whites and cream. This version is the one which you are most likely to find in restaurants in France. Quenelles were popular with the Edwardians, who served them as a garnish rather than as a main dish. Make them well in advance and freeze them for an impressive but trouble-free main course.

To make the quenelles, pour the milk over the breadcrumbs in a bowl and leave them to soak. Cut the butter into cubes and keep it somewhere warm so that it becomes soft but does not melt. Cube the salmon and chop it as finely as possible in a food processor, or a blender. Take handfuls of the breadcrumbs and squeeze out the surplus milk, then add them to the fish in the processor. Process again. Add the butter and process for a third time, then add the seasonings, the egg and the yolks, one at a time, stopping when you have a uniformly smooth, pale pinkish-yellow, fairly firm paste. Taste to check the seasoning – it is delicious raw. (You may have to do this in two or three batches, depending on the size of your processor or blender.) Place the mixture in the fridge for a few hours to firm up. Sprinkle a board lightly with flour, take heaped dessertspoonfuls of the quenelle mixture and form them into small sausage shapes. They can be frozen at this point, packed in boxes and layered with baking parchment. When you come to cook them, half-fill a shallow sauté pan with a mixture of fish-stock and white wine and bring it to the boil. Add the quenelles, bring back to a simmer and

simmer over a medium heat for 15 minutes, turning them over at half-time. Remove them with a draining spoon and place in a warmed, buttered gratin dish.

To make the sauce, remove the toughest stalks from the sorrel, wash it and tear the leaves up a little, then put them in a small pan with the butter. Cook gently with the lid on the pan for about 5 minutes, then stir the sorrel into a purée. Add the flour and stir well, then pour on the hot fish stock, stirring constantly. Bring to the boil, stirring all the time, then lower the heat and simmer gently for about 10 minutes. Add the cream, season with salt, pepper and a little nutmeg, and pour over the quenelles. Sprinkle with breadcrumbs and brown in a hot oven or under the grill until bubbling.

Serve this with plain boiled rice, or simply with baby carrots cooked and then tossed in a little butter, together with the bits of asparagus left from the consommé, cut into centimetre lengths.

As this is a delicate creamy dish, a crisp green salad of seasonal leaves afterwards is particularly suitable.

Strawberry Meringue Cream

450g (1lb) fresh strawberries
4 meringues, broken into
*   smallish pieces*
300ml (½pt) whipping cream
300ml (½pt) fromage frais
2 tablespoons vanilla sugar
flaked almonds, toasted

Hull and slice the strawberries. Whip the cream and fromage frais together, sweetening the mixture with the vanilla sugar, then fold in the meringue pieces and strawberry slices. Pile into a decorative glass bowl and scatter the top with toasted flaked almonds. This should not be made too far ahead as the strawberries will 'weep' into the cream.

Strawberries Romanof

1kg (2lb) fresh strawberries
juice of 3 large oranges, strained
miniature bottle or
*   3 tablespoons orange liqueur*

Another Edwardian favourite, for which you need an orange liqueur, such as curaçao, or Cointreau. It is a good accompaniment to the strawberry cream, or can be served separately.

Quarter the strawberries and place in a decorative bowl. Pour over the orange juice and liqueur. Chill for a minimum of 2 hours.

Scotney Cricket Tea

Club Tie Sandwiches
Cucumber Sandwiches
Cricket Pads
Century Cake
Howzat Ice-cream
Iced Tea

This menu for tea includes some suitably traditional sandwiches, sponge cakes called Cricket Pads, a Century Cake, and green-and white ice-cream studded with cricket ball-like maraschino cherries.

Club Tie Sandwiches

large fine-sliced white or
    multi-grain loaf
100g (4oz) softened butter
8 shelled hard-boiled eggs
jar black lumpfish roe
jar red lumpfish roe
6 tablespoons mayonnaise
squeeze lemon juice
halved cherry tomatoes and
    black olives to garnish

Makes about forty sandwiches.
Put the halved hard-boiled eggs and the mayonnaise into a food processor and process to a coarse paste, seasoning with a squeeze of lemon juice. Using a fork, mix in the two colours of lumpfish roe until they are well distributed. Spread all the slices of bread with the butter, then spread half the slices with the egg paste and put the two together, then cut into triangles, or squares. Remove the crusts if you like. Garnish with the olives and tomatoes to continue the colour scheme.

Cucumber Sandwiches

large fine-sliced brown loaf
100–170g (4–6oz) softened
    butter
1–2 cucumbers
about 1 teaspoon salt

Makes about forty sandwiches.
With a potato peeler, remove the cucumber peel in alternate stripes down the length of the cucumbers, then slice them as finely as possible, using a mandolin or the appropriate disc of the food processor. Sprinkle with the salt and leave in a colander to drain for at least 30 minutes. Rinse the cucumber under the cold tap, drain and dry on paper towels. Use to make up the sandwiches in the usual way. Garnish with parsley.

Cricket Pads

225g (8oz) each soft margarine,
 caster sugar and self-raising
 flour
4 eggs
½ teaspoon vanilla extract

FOR THE ICING

125g (4oz) unsalted butter
250g (8oz) sifted icing sugar
squeeze lemon juice
4 squares chocolate, plain
 or milk, melted

Makes twenty-four 'pads'.

Grease and flour lightly two 20 × 30cm (8 × 12in) Swiss roll tins and preheat the oven to 175°C/350°F/Gas 4. Beat together the margarine and sugar until pale and creamy, then beat in the eggs, one at a time, each accompanied by a sprinkling of the flour. Add the vanilla extract (preferably *not* vanilla essence) and beat again, then sift the remaining flour over the mixture and fold it in lightly. Divide the mixture between the two tins and bake for about 25 minutes (less in a fan-oven) until lightly browned and springy to the touch. Turn out and cool on wire racks.

To ice, cream together the butter, sugar and lemon juice and spread as smoothly as possible over the two cakes. Cut each cake in half lengthways, then each half across at 5cm (2in) intervals, so that each cake is cut into 12 'cricket pads'. To mark the 'pads' divisions, dip the tip of a wooden skewer into the melted chocolate and draw lines down the length of each 'pad'.

Century Cake

300ml (½pt) medium-strong
 strained tea
170g (6oz) sultanas
170g (6oz) currants
125g (4oz) raisins
225g (8oz) pale soft brown
 sugar
225g (8oz) soft margarine,
 or unsalted butter
3 eggs
275g (10oz) self-raising flour
50g (2oz) ground almonds
grated rind 1 orange

This is an old-fashioned 'boiled' fruit cake, moist and delicious and a favourite in our family whatever the occasion. For a cricket tea I would decorate it with the appropriate score cut out of marzipan and stuck on the top with a few brush strokes of apricot jam.

This quantity makes enough to fill a 26cm (10in) cake tin, which cuts into 12 slices. For the average cricket tea you will need to make two, and they are best made at least a week in advance, to mature to a proper fruity richness.

Put the tea and the dried fruit into a pan, bring to the boil, cover and simmer for about 5 minutes, then leave to stand overnight, or until cold. Preheat the oven to 175°C/350°F/ Gas 4. Grease and line a 26cm (10in) cake tin with a removable base. Cream together the butter or margarine, sugar and grated orange rind, then beat in the eggs one at a time, each accompanied by a sprinkling of the flour. Stir in the

soaked fruit, then fold in the flour and the ground almonds, mixed together. Transfer the mixture to the cake tin and bake for 1½ hours, then lower the heat and bake for a further half-hour at 160°C/325°F/Gas 3, or until the mixture has shrunk from the sides of the tin. If using a fan oven, bake at 150°C/300°F/Gas 2 for 1 hour, then lower the heat to 140°C/275°F/Gas 1 and bake for a further 20 minutes. Leave to cool in the tin for 15 minutes, then turn out and finish cooling on a wire rack. When cold, wrap well in layers of greaseproof paper and cling film to keep a week or more. To decorate, cut numbers from marzipan rolled out to a 5mm (¼in) thickness and have them ready for whenever tea is served, together with a pot of apricot jam and a pastry brush with which to stick them on the cake.

Howzat Ice-cream

2 x 750ml (1¼pt) cartons vanilla ice-cream
750ml (1¼pt) carton mint (or pistachio) ice-cream
2 jars maraschino cherries

You can make your own ice-cream, of course, *and* poach fresh cherries in a light syrup, but this version is both quicker and cheaper.

Drain the cherries of their syrup. Turn out the cartons of ice-cream and slice each of the vanilla ones in half horizontally. Slice the green ice-cream into three sections. Layer the slices, alternately green and white, dotting each layer with the cherries before adding the next. Using a piece of baking parchment, press down each layer before adding the next, so that the cherries become embedded. Sandwich this ice-cream tower between two plates and chill in the freezer, then remove the top plate and decorate with more cherry cricket balls before serving.

Iced Tea

There is nothing more refreshing or reviving than tea, and iced tea on a hot day is perfection. It might be a good idea to offer two sorts – a pale scented infusion of Lapsang Suchong with slices of lemon, and a stronger brew of Ceylon (for soft-water areas) or Assam (for medium to hard-water areas),

aromatised with orange slices and a cinnamon stick or two. Approximately two dozen cups of tea-with-milk can be extracted from 125g (4oz) leaf tea, but as iced tea is served weaker, you will need only 175g (6oz) for 48 wine glasses.

Make the tea extra strong, using only a quarter as much water as normal and leave it to brew for about 10 minutes, then strain into large jugs. Add your chosen flavourings, then top up with cold water until about the right strength, and add ice cubes to chill it further. Garnish with sprigs of mint and keep the jugs in the fridge. Made in this way the tea will cool far more quickly and will have a fresher flavour, and you can make more as needed, provided you have a good supply of ice-cubes. If you like, you can have a few jugs of 'spritzer' tea, using sparkling mineral water to top up the jugs. And always offer something stronger for those who refuse to believe that tea is sufficient for a winning team.

Felbrigg Ballooning Snacks

Ramekins of Potted Fish or Meat
Tomato Baskets of Vegetables
Black-stuffed Peppers
Herb Cheese Panniers
Heavenly Mouthfuls
Passing Clouds
Champagne

for four

These are for eating at any time of day, in case your ballooning trip is cancelled and you need to.eat for solace, or you were too nervous to eat beforehand. The theme is one of containers, and you can include all of these for a very special occasion or just choose one or two.

Ramekins of Potted Fish or Meat

350g (12oz) cooked meat (ham, beef [see page 43], game, chicken) or cooked smoked fish (haddock, trout, hot-smoked salmon)
175g (6oz) good quality butter, such as Normandy or Dutch
salt, pepper
few drops of Tabasco or Worcester sauce
pinch grated nutmeg or powdered mace
squeeze lemon juice
extra butter to seal – see method
herbs to garnish – see method

These can be made up to 4 days ahead and stored in the fridge. An assortment of fish and meat adds to the variety and will suit any fish-eating vegetarians in the party.

Remove any fat or gristle from the meat, and any skin and bones from the fish. Process meat or fish in a food processor with the butter until a smooth paste, then season to taste with salt and freshly ground pepper and some of the other seasonings. I like to use Tabasco and mace for fish, nutmeg and Worcester sauce for meat and poultry, but all benefit from some lemon juice. Divide mixture between 4 small ramekins and smooth the tops to just below the rim. Melt the butter over a low heat, then leave to stand in a warm place for about 10 minutes. Strain through a coffee filter paper or new J-cloth dipped in hot water and pour over the surface of each ramekin to seal out the air. Press a herb in the centre so that you can tell which is meat and which fish: parsley for the former, fennel for the latter, for example. Serve with crisp oatcakes or pitta bread.

Tomato Baskets of Vegetables

8–12 tomatoes, depending on size
350g–450g (12oz–1lb) of a mixture of summer vegetables, such as french beans, peas, new potatoes, asparagus, fresh sweet corn, courgettes
about 300ml (½pt) mayonnaise
2–3 teaspoons balsamic vinegar
6 large leaves of fresh basil
1 fat clove of garlic, poached until soft in a little boiling water

Avoid those hefty tasteless beef tomatoes and pick a smaller 'Grown for flavour' variety, which you can eat in your fingers.

Cook the vegetables until just tender – they do not develop their subtle cooked flavours if too underdone – then dice or slice them small. Add the balsamic vinegar, the cooked garlic and the basil, torn into little bits, to the mayonnaise, then add the vegetables. Cover and leave to stand while you prepare the tomatoes. Wash and dry them and remove a slice from the stalk end. Using a sharp pointed knife, remove the flesh and seeds from the insides and sprinkle with a little salt. Leave them to drain upside-down on a plate for about 30 minutes, before filling each with the vegetable and mayonnaise filling. Replace the lids and pack upright for safe transportation, filling any gaps in between with crumpled kitchen paper. Take olive ciabatta bread or rolls to eat with them.

Black-stuffed Peppers

4 large red peppers
225g (8oz) cooked brown rice
tin anchovy fillets, finely
 chopped
100g (4oz) black olives, finely
 chopped
12 raisins, soaked in hot water
 and finely chopped
6 large fresh basil leaves
1 teaspoon tomato purée (or use
 the pulp from the middle of
 the stuffed tomatoes, if
 making both dishes)
6 tablespoons extra virgin olive
 oil
2 cloves garlic, finely chopped
salt and freshly ground black
 pepper
pinch allspice

To continue the container theme the peppers should be kept upright, with a lid cut from the stalk end. However, I find eating them in the fingers much easier if they have been cut in half lengthways, so that they form boats rather than baskets, but the choice is yours.

Wash and halve the peppers (or take lids from the stem end). Remove the cores and the bulk of the seeds, there is no need to remove them all as they have a pleasantly nutty flavour that is only faintly hot and I often include several in the dish I am making. Grill the peppers under a hot grill, turning them as the skin begins to blacken and blister. Wrap in cling film and leave until they are cool enough to handle, then remove the skin. Heat the oven to 175°C/350°F/Gas 4. Pour a thin film of olive oil over the base of a shallow oven dish and arrange the peppers in it. Make the stuffing by combining the finely chopped olives and anchovies (and their oil) and raisins with the rice, adding the tomato purée or pulp, the torn basil leaves, garlic and seasonings. Mix well together and stuff the peppers, heaping the filling up generously. Dribble the remaining olive oil over the peppers and their stuffing and bake for 30 minutes. Delicious hot or warm, as well as cold.

Herb Cheese Panniers

1 French loaf
1 garlic-and-herb flavoured
 soft cheese
2 tablespoons finely chopped
 fresh herbs –tarragon, basil,
 chervil, chives, parsley, all
 or some of these
4 tablespoons olive oil or about
 50g (2oz) butter, melted

Preheat the oven to 200°C/400°F/Gas 6. Cut the loaf across into 8 slices about 5cm (2in) thick and take a 'core' from the centre of each slice. Mix the herbs with the olive oil or butter (I prefer the lighter finish the oil gives). Brush each slice of bread all over the cut surfaces with the herb and oil or butter mixture and arrange on a baking sheet. Bake in the centre of the oven for about 10 minutes, or until lightly golden and crisp. Transfer to a wire rack and leave to cool. Fill the centres with the soft cheese. Serve with whole cherry tomatoes.

Heavenly Mouthfuls

2 small charentais melons
3 ripe passion fruit
300ml ($\frac{1}{2}$pt) whipping cream
150ml ($\frac{1}{4}$pt) fromage frais
1 teaspoon orange flower water
    (optional)
caster sugar

Halve the passion fruit and scoop out the flesh and seeds; push through a sieve. Whip the cream until billowy but not too stiff, then fold in the fromage frais and the passion fruit purée. Sweeten to taste then add the orange flower water if using. Halve the melons and scoop out the seeds. Remove some of the flesh and dice it fairly small. With a sharp knife, cut a zig-zag edge to each half-melon. Pile the melon flesh back into the shells, keeping back some to use as a garnish, then spoon the passion fruit cream on top. Garnish with some of the melon dice and keep cold. Serve with sponge fingers.

Passing Clouds

whites of 4 eggs
120g (4$\frac{1}{2}$oz) caster sugar
450ml (15fl oz) milk
350g (12oz) gooseberries,
    topped and tailed
1 tablespoon elderflower cordial
300ml ($\frac{1}{2}$pt) whipping cream
silver balls (optional)

These are served in ramekins, so do not choose this dessert if you are using ramekins for potted meat or fish. The poached meringue 'clouds' float on a base of gooseberry fool and are powdered with silver balls to represent raindrops – but these are optional.

Stew the gooseberries very gently, with the elderflower cordial and 75g (3oz) of the sugar. When soft, purée in a blender or processor and leave to cool. Whip the egg whites until foamy, add 10g ($\frac{1}{2}$oz) sugar and continue to whisk until stiff, then fold in the last 25g (1oz) sugar. Bring the milk to a boil in a wide shallow pan (a heavy frying pan will do), then reduce to a simmer. Poach tablespoonfuls of the meringue mixture in the milk until firm. This will take about half a minute and the 'clouds' should be turned once during cooking. Lift out with a perforated spoon and drain on a plate. Whip the cream and fold it in to the gooseberry purée. Fill each ramekin two-thirds full with the fool and top with a 'cloud', then scatter with a few silver balls, if using.

A Portable Winter Sporting Lunch

Spiced Tomato and Sherry Soup
Leek- or Game-filled Baked Potatoes
Apple and Mincemeat Crumble with Apple Brandy Butter
Cheese, Oatcakes and Celery

for six

At the turn of the century such a lunch would have been transported, sometimes even cooked, in a hay-box. Now we have insulated picnic bags and boxes, and thermos flasks. Hot-water bottles placed at the bottom of insulated boxes should keep the baked potatoes and the apple crumble warm, but it is best to wrap them well in polythene bags to stop the food tasting of hot rubber. Well packed, this menu should be able to withstand being jolted about in a vehicle driven over tracks and fields.

Spiced Tomato and Sherry Soup

3 tins chopped tomatoes
1 large mild onion
2 tablespoons groundnut
or sunflower oil
sprig rosemary and 1 bayleaf
2 cloves garlic
3 tablespoons tomato ketchup
1 tablespoon paprika
2 spicy vegetable stock cubes
1–2 tablespoons brown sugar
salt and pepper
3 sherry glasses medium
dry sherry

This is also perfect for Bonfire Night, quick and cheap to make but full of warming flavours. I suggest using vegetable stock cubes so that it can be offered to vegetarians, but a beef stock cube with a dash of Worcester sauce works well.

Chop the onion finely and put it, together with the rosemary and bayleaf, in a heavy pan with the oil over a low heat. Sprinkle with a little salt to draw out the moisture, put the lid on the pan and leave to soften for about 10 minutes. Add the sliced garlic, the paprika, tinned tomatoes and tomato ketchup and cook for a further 5 minutes. Add 3 tomato tins of water, the crumbled stock cubes and a grinding of pepper and leave to simmer gently for about 25 minutes. Cool a little, remove the herbs and then liquidize or process until less lumpy, but not too smooth. Return to the pan, add the sugar to taste and the sherry. Bring up to boiling point and pour into the flasks. If you want to evaporate all the alcohol, in the interests of those who have to drive, simmer the soup for about 10 minutes after adding the sherry. Serve with buttered brown rolls.

Leek- or Game-filled Baked Potatoes

Allow 1 large or 1½ medium baking potatoes per person – I prefer King Edwards, but any good floury potato will do. Scrub the potatoes and pierce each with a metal skewer (or impale them on a potato baker) to cut down the baking time. Bake at 200°C/400°F/Gas 6 for about 1½ hours for the large size, 1 hour for the medium size.

When the potatoes are done, cut them in half horizontally and scoop out the insides to make a sizeable hollow, but leaving a nice wall of potato within the skin. Rough this up with a fork, then spoon in your chosen filling. Put each filled half potato on a piece of foil and pinch the edges tightly together at the top. Keep the potatoes warm in the oven until ready to transport. If making ahead, cool the potatoes and their filling, then reheat, fill and wrap. These are easiest eaten with spoons, but the remaining skins can be eaten with fingers.

LEEK FILLING

450g (1lb) cleaned and sliced leeks
500ml (1pt) hot milk, flavoured with a bayleaf
60g (2½oz) butter
60g (2½oz) flour
175g (6oz) mature Cheddar cheese
2 tablespoons coarse grain mustard
salt and pepper

Steam the leeks until tender, then drain. Make a cheese sauce by stirring the flour into the melted butter, adding the hot milk gradually, and stirring all the time over a low heat until the sauce thickens. Simmer gently, stirring from time to time, for about 15 minutes, then add the cheese and stir until this has melted completely. Take out the bayleaf and stir in the leeks and the mustard. Check the seasoning and add more salt if needed – much will depend on how salty the cheese is. Press cling film over the surface to prevent a skin forming. If you are making this in advance, the mixture can be cooled and reheated. If using straight away, keep it warm in a low oven or over hot water.

*about 1kg (2–2¼lb) boneless
    game – venison, hare, pigeon,
    pheasant, rabbit, some or
    all of these
300ml (½pt) hot stock from
    the game bones
2 tablespoons olive oil
2 onions, finely sliced
2 carrots, diced
2 sticks celery, diced
salt and pepper
4 crushed juniper berries
generous glass red wine
2 tablespoons mushroom
    ketchup
3 tablespoons flour*

This is basically a game stew and like any such dish is all the better for being made a day or two ahead and reheated.

Season the meat with salt, freshly ground pepper and the crushed juniper berries, then brown it all over in the hot oil, in two batches if necessary, and set aside. In the same pan, cook the vegetables for about 10 minutes, stirring occasionally, until they are beginning to colour. Stir in the flour, then the hot stock and bring to the boil, stirring hard. Put the meat into an ovenproof casserole, add the vegetables and their thickened stock, the wine and mushroom ketchup. Either simmer over a low heat on the hob for about 1½ hours, until the meat is tender, or cook in a low (160°C/325°F/Gas 3) oven for about 2 hours. The sauce should be thick, slightly thicker than you would want for an ordinary stew. If it is too thin, thicken it by adding a dessertspoonful of cornflour diluted with more stock or wine.

Apple and Mincemeat Crumble

*3 large cooking apples, peeled,
    cored and sliced
6 Cox's Orange apples, peeled,
    cored and sliced
85g (3oz) pale brown sugar
approx. 225g (8oz) mincemeat
juice 1 orange*

FOR THE CRUMBLE TOPPING
*225g (8oz) plain flour
100g (4oz) unsalted butter
100g (4oz) demerara sugar
50g (2oz) finely chopped
    walnuts (optional)
1 teaspoon cinnamon*

The apples sit on a bed of mincemeat, for a more robust version of an old favourite. The chopped walnuts give the crumble topping extra zest, but are optional.

Preheat the oven to 175°C/350°F/Gas 4. Either rub the butter into the flour until it looks like fine breadcrumbs, then add the sugar, walnuts and cinnamon, or process butter, flour, spice and sugar in a food processor and add the walnuts. Spoon the mincemeat over the bottom of a baking dish to make a thick bed. Toss the apple slices with the sugar and spread them on top, then add the orange juice and spoon the crumble topping over. Bake for 30 minutes. Serve warm, or reheated, with the Apple Brandy Butter.

Apple Brandy Butter

175g (6oz) unsalted butter
90g (3½oz) pale soft brown
  sugar
grated rind and juice of ½ lemon
2 tablespoons calvados or
  English apple brandy

Soften the butter a little, then put it in the liquidizer or processor with the brown sugar and lemon rind. Process until light and fluffy. Mix the calvados or apple brandy with the lemon juice and add it in a thin stream through the lid with the motor running, as if you were making a mayonnaise. Scoop into a pot, cover and store in the fridge until needed.

Cheese, Oatcakes and Celery

For the cheese, I would pick a fine piece of Stilton, a good wedge of farmhouse Cheddar or Double Gloucester, and serve them with oatcakes and sticks of crisp celery. Clementines or satsumas are also nice as they are easily peeled and not too messy. As a finale serve coffee and good quality plain chocolate.

FEASTING THE COMMUNITY

FEASTING THE COMMUNITY

The histories of great houses are dotted with records of public festivities. At *Stowe*, in Buckinghamshire, during the 1790s, a rollicking supper for the tenant farmers was held annually in honour of Lady Buckingham's birthday; the archives at *Cotehele*, in Cornwall, have an account of a tenants' dinner in 1830. Long before Mrs Greville's time at *Polesden Lacey*, Richard Sheridan, the playwright, who bought the estate in 1797, held harvest festivals there. In a delightful record of years spent at *Selworthy*, Somerset, in the 1850s, the rector's daughter remembers preparations at the rectory for the tithe dinners: 'It was a sight worth seeing – one great joint roasting before the big kitchen fire, and in a great back-kitchen another huge joint was roasting, the spit being turned by the old basket-maker.'

A well-known Rowlandson print depicts the ample figures of the local populace feasting under the trees at *Ham House*, Surrey, and at *Petworth House* in Sussex the 3rd Earl of Egremont was famously hospitable, holding annual feasts for his tenants and workers throughout the severe agricultural recession of the 1830s. William Frederick Witherington, whose painting *Fête in Petworth Park*, hangs in the North Gallery, was a good deal kinder to the revellers than Rowlandson, or perhaps he wished to flatter his patron by depicting them as graceful rather than lumpen. At *Knightshayes*, in Devon, the first Sir John Heathcote-Amory held summer outings for the workers from his lace-making factory in Tiverton. These works' outings were the continuation of a long history of 'beanfeasts' (later shortened to 'beanos') given by employers for their workforces.

Our modern equivalents are no less rollicking, but perhaps rather less paternalistic. We celebrate with street parties, village hot-pot suppers, harvest festival dinners, often in aid of a good cause.

For such occasions you need food that is easily cooked in large quantities, using simple recipes so that they can be batch-cooked in individual kitchens. This means baked, rather than roast, meats. An ox-roast is definitely best left to the professionals, who know how to end up with meat that is cooked through, rather than singed on the outside and raw in the middle.

Such dishes as hot-pots and casseroles are ideal, and now there must be a vegetarian option, although, once upon a time, a feast without meat would not have

been considered a feast. In the autumn nothing is more festive than a pumpkin and corn casserole served from hollowed-out pumpkins, in summer cold dishes such as stuffed vegetables, or pasta dishes, can be infinitely variable and delicious, although not traditionally British.

All quantities in these menus are for 10 people, but can easily be doubled, or cooked in batches.

Harvest Festival

Herb-crusted Baked Chicken
Tomato, Courgette and Pasta Casserole
Crusty Brown Rolls and Butter
Assorted Salads
Fresh Fruit Pyramids
Harvest Cake and Cheese

for ten

Herb-crusted Baked Chicken

20 chicken thigh joints
grated rind and juice of 2 lemons
4 teaspoons herbes de Provence
4 cloves garlic, crushed
4 tablespoons groundnut
  or sunflower oil
175g (6oz) fresh brown
  breadcrumbs
large handful parsley
salt and pepper
extra groundnut or sunflower
  oil for basting

Mix together the lemon juice, groundnut oil, herbes de Provence and garlic and toss the chicken joints in this mixture, so that they are well coated. Cover and refrigerate overnight. Next day, process the breadcrumbs with the lemon rind and parsley, salt and pepper. Preheat the oven to 200°C/400°F/Gas 6. Arrange the joints in two baking tins – allowing a little space between each joint – and spread the breadcrumb mixture evenly over them, pressing the crumbs down firmly. Dribble a little oil over the top, then bake for 45 minutes. Serve with the tomato, courgette and pasta casserole.

Tomato, Courgette and Pasta Casserole

675g (1½lb) wholewheat pasta
    shells
1kg (2lb) courgettes
4 x 425g (14oz) tins chopped
    tomatoes
1 large mild onion
4 cloves garlic, finely chopped
bunch of flavouring herbs –
    marjoram, parsley, thyme,
    sage, bayleaf, celery stalk,
    strip orange peel
1 teaspoon sugar
4 tablespoons olive oil
bunch fresh basil

This can be served as an accompaniment to the chicken or as a vegetarian option. I use tins of chopped tomatoes as the flavour is better, but if you have access to plenty of cheap, flavourful fresh tomatoes, they will do just as well – but they do need skinning!

Soften the sliced onion in the olive oil, with a sprinkling of salt to draw out the moisture, for about 10 minutes. Add the garlic, the tomatoes and the bunch of herbs, season with salt and freshly ground pepper and simmer gently for about 30 minutes. (If using fresh tomatoes simmer for a further 15 minutes.) Meanwhile, cut the courgettes into coarse strips and cook in boiling salted water for a minute, then drain. Cook the pasta as directed on the packet and drain. When the sauce is ready, add the sugar, check the seasoning, take out the herbs, add the courgettes and cook for a further 10 minutes, or until the courgettes are soft, then add the pasta. If making ahead, cool at this point, then reheat just before serving, adding the finely torn-up basil leaves so they release their wonderful scent as the casserole is served. Offer baskets of crusty brown rolls and plenty of butter with this.

Assorted Salads

The salads to accompany these dishes can be whatever is cheaply available at the time. Possibilities include runner bean and tomato salad, the beans cooked until just tender and dressed with a vinaigrette while they are still warm, a mixed green salad decorated with nasturtium and marigold flowers which look wonderful and taste good, and raw courgette and mushroom salad seasoned with chopped chives and marjoram.

Fresh Fruit Pyramids

At this time of year English fruit is good and looks wonderful piled high on decorative dishes so that people can help themselves – arranged in opulent piles nothing so clearly shows off this glorious season of plenty. Early varieties of apples, such as Discovery and, if you are lucky, Beauty of Bath, look wonderful arranged with plums and greengages. If you have them, you can add late summer raspberries, strawberries and currants and early blackberries to your displays. And why not stretch a point and include the imported nectarines and peaches which are so cheap at this time of year? Use large leaves, such as vine or currant, to form a base for the pyramids.

Harvest Cake and Cheese

450g (1lb) plain flour
225g (8oz) softened butter
225g (8oz) pale soft brown
  sugar
225g (8oz) currants
3 eggs
300ml ($\frac{1}{2}$pt) milk
2 teaspoons baking powder
1 teaspoon grated nutmeg

Basic fruit cakes using only the cheapest dried fruit, currants, were taken out to the fields to fortify the harvesting teams. But 'Common Pound Cake', as it was also known, is very good indeed, and delicious with English cheese. Ideally the cheese should be fairly local and this is more possible than it was: Lancashire, Cheshire, Wensleydale, Cheddar, Double Gloucester and Caerphilly are still being made in their localities and there are a number of 'new' cheeses too, such as Cornish Yarg, Surrey Old Scotland Farm, Devon Garland and Lanark Blue.

Line a 25cm (10in) cake tin with a removable base, and preheat the oven to 170°C/350°F/Gas 4. Cream the butter and sugar and add the eggs, and a sprinkling of flour, one a time, beating well. Mix the rest of the flour with the currants and nutmeg and fold in, then add the baking powder to the milk and stir into the mixture. Spoon into the cake tin, level off the top and bake for about $1\frac{3}{4}$ hours – a skewer pushed into the centre should come out clean when the cake is done. If using a fan oven, reduce the temperature given above by 10°C and the cooking time by about 20 minutes.

Hallowe'en Supper

Pumpkin, Corn and Sausage Cauldron
Baked Herb Potatoes
Seeded Loaves and Butter
Red Salad
Plum and Walnut Pie

for ten

This menu would also be a good alternative Harvest Festival celebration.

Pumpkin, Corn and Sausage Cauldron

1 large pumpkin, weighing about 2−2·5kg (4−5lb)
675g (1½lb) pumpkin flesh, cut into large cubes
4 fresh corn-cobs, or 450g (1lb) frozen sweet corn
450g (1lb) waxy potatoes, peeled and cubed
20 spicy chipolata sausages
1 large mild onion, diced
3 cloves garlic, finely chopped
2 teaspoons powdered cumin
3 teaspoons powdered coriander
600ml (1pt) tomato passata
1 l (1¾pt) spicy vegetable stock
groundnut oil
salt and freshly ground pepper

For this recipe you will need a large orange fairy-tale pumpkin as your serving 'cauldron'. As a vegetarian version, substitute 2 tins of red kidney beans and a dessertspoonful of paprika for the sausages.

Cut a lid from the pumpkin and hollow it out, leaving a lining of flesh inside the skin. Brush all over the inside with a little groundnut oil. Stand it on a baking sheet and bake for about 45 minutes at 160°C/325°F/Gas 3. After 30 minutes check that it has not become too soft or it will collapse. Keep warm if using immediately, or set aside to cool if cooking ahead.

Soften the onion in a couple of tablespoonfuls of groundnut oil, together with the cumin and coriander, then add the garlic, tomato passata and half the vegetable stock, plus a grinding of pepper. Simmer this steadily for 15 minutes. Add the cubed potato and the pumpkin and cook for a further 20 minutes. Meanwhile, scrape the raw kernels from the corn-cobs (the sweetness of fresh corn is so delicious it is worth taking this extra trouble; if using frozen corn, add a teaspoon of sugar as well), and grill the sausages until nicely brown. Add both sausages and corn and cook gently for another 30 minutes, by which time the pumpkin will have dissolved to thicken the sauce. Keep checking the level of liquid and adding some of the remaining hot stock – the stew

should be just liquid, not swimmingly so. Add salt and freshly ground pepper to taste at the end (salt hardens the sweet corn if added before it is cooked). Spoon the hot stew into the warmed pumpkin shell and replace the lid. If there is too much stew, keep it hot and add it later.

Baked Herbed Potatoes

10 medium baking potatoes
olive or groundnut oil
4 cloves garlic, finely chopped
large bunch parsley, finely
    chopped
tablespoon herbes de Provence
sea salt and pepper

Allow a medium potato per person.

Cut the potatoes in half lengthways and score the flesh deeply with a sharp knife. Arrange the halves on two baking sheets. Sprinkle with sea salt, the herbes de Provence, and dribble about a teaspoonful of oil over each. Bake at 200°C/ 400°F/Gas 6 for the first 25 minutes, then lower the heat to 175°C/350°F/Gas 4 for another 20 minutes or until soft. Meanwhile, mix together the garlic and parsley and add just enough oil to moisten. When the potatoes are done, fork up the flesh and work some of the parsley mixture into each one. Return to the oven just long enough to brown the tops – or do this under the grill. If cooking ahead, cool after forking up the centres. About 35 minutes before serving, add the parsley mixture and reheat and brown the tops in a hot oven for 30 minutes.

Seeded Loaves

Serve a variety of seed-covered breads with this feast: sesame, sunflower, poppy seed. If such bread is not available, brush french sticks with oil and sprinkle with the various seeds, then warm in the oven.

Red Salad

Finely shred carrots and raw beetroot, and toss in a vinaigrette with some radicchio and any of the red-tinged lettuces now available. Add strips of red pepper, softened and skinned as described on page 22, and seeded and skinned tomatoes. Garnish with bright red nasturtium flowers.

Plum and Walnut Pie

FOR THE PASTRY

350g (12oz) plain flour
3 dessertspoons icing sugar
175g (6oz) butter and/or hard margarine
squeeze lemon juice
2 tablespoons (approx.) cold milk to mix

FOR THE FILLING

900g (2lb) plums, halved and stoned
100g (4oz) walnut pieces
40g (1½oz) unsalted butter
100g (4oz) soft brown sugar
½ teaspoon cinnamon
milk
granulated sugar

This is a lovely, rich and spicy pie, a nice change from apple and even more quickly made. Bake it in a deep 25cm (10in) flan tin with a removable base and serve with slightly sweetened whipped cream.

Make the pastry by rubbing the fat into the flour, with a squeeze of lemon juice, then stirring in the icing sugar. Add enough cold milk to mix to a firm dough (if making this in a food processor, you will probably need less milk than if making it by hand). Leave the pastry to rest in a cool place while you assemble the filling. Mix the plum halves with the sugar, cinnamon and walnuts (chop these smaller if they are large, they will then distribute better among the fruit). Roll out the pastry and line the flan tin, leaving plenty of overlap to fold over the fruit. Heat the oven to 190°C/375°F/Gas 5 and put a baking sheet on a middle shelf. Pile the fruit in the middle of the pastry-lined flan tin and dot with the butter, then fold the pastry up over the fruit; there will be an area of uncovered fruit in the centre. Brush the pastry top with milk and sprinkle with a little granulated sugar. Bake for 35 minutes, until the pastry is nicely brown and the fruit soft. When the pie has cooled, stand the tin on an upturned jam jar and gently remove the flan ring. Leaving the pie on the base will help it to arrive safely at the feast.

Summer Street Party or Village Beanfeast

Broad Bean and Potato Soup
Immense Sausage Roll
Immense Mushroom, Rice and Spinach Roll
Summer Puddings

for ten

Broad Bean and Potato Soup

900g (2lb) scraped new
    potatoes, cubed
900g (2lb) podded broad beans
2 bunches spring onions,
    trimmed and finely sliced
2l (3½pt) vegetable stock
150ml (¼pt) single cream
2 tablespoons finely chopped
    parsley
40g (1½oz) butter
salt and pepper

For centuries the broad bean has been the centre of 'bean-feasts', and in spite of the fact that the frozen bean is in season year round this is a summer soup. It is thick and filling, a beautiful green and white and flecked with parsley, the traditional accompaniment to broad beans. Use frozen beans if these are cheaper than fresh. This recipe will suit vegetarians.

Melt the butter in a large pan and add the potatoes and a little salt. Cook gently without browning for about 5 minutes, then add the beans, stirring well to mix them with the potatoes, and cook for a further minute before adding the onions and pouring on the stock. Bring to the boil, add salt and pepper and simmer gently for about 15 minutes – do not overcook the vegetables, but make sure they are tender. Add the cream and reheat to just below boiling, then stir in the parsley. Serve with crusty brown bread.

Immense Sausage Roll

FOR THE PASTRY

350g (12oz) plain flour
1½ teaspoons baking powder
175g (6oz) hard margarine
50g (2oz) vegetable lard
½ teaspoon salt

FOR THE FILLING

1kg (2¼lb) sausage meat
finely chopped parsley and sage
4 tablespoons coarse grain
    mustard
1 egg, beaten

This is very easy to make and tremendous fun for a street party, or any celebration laid out on long tables. Each person makes a sausage roll for 10 and these are joined up along the length of the table. The vegetarian version has a mushroom, rice and spinach stuffing instead of sausage meat, and you can alternate the two, but be careful to decorate them so that it is clear which is which.

Make up the pastry as on page 149 and leave to rest for 30 minutes. Break up the sausage meat and work in the fresh herbs – these will make all the difference to the flavour. Heat the oven to 200°C/400°F/Gas 6, and line a baking sheet with baking parchment. Roll two-thirds of the pastry into an oblong and spread the centre with half the mustard. Shape the sausage meat into a long sausage and place it on the pastry, then roll out the remaining pastry and spread with the rest of the mustard, and place it, mustard side down, on top of the sausage meat. Trim the pastry base all

round to within 2cm (¾in) of the sausage meat and brush a line of beaten egg round the meat, then pinch top and bottom together firmly to make a good seal. Roll out the pastry trimmings and cut out 'S' shapes. Stick these shapes down the spine of the sausage roll with beaten egg, to make a decorative pattern and denote that this is the sausage version. Make a few cuts in the pastry to let out the steam, and brush all over with the remaining egg. Bake for 45 minutes, covering the pastry if it gets too brown.

Immense Mushroom, Rice and Spinach Roll

PASTRY:

ingredients as opposite, see method page 149

FOR THE FILLING

350g (12oz) mushrooms, finely sliced
150g (5oz) brown rice
1 large onion, finely chopped
450g (1lb) fresh spinach, or 225g (8oz) frozen
2 cloves garlic, finely chopped
1 dessertspoon crushed coriander seeds
2 teaspoons powdered cumin
salt and freshly ground pepper
vegetable stock or water
2 tablespoons groundnut oil

Make up the pastry and leave to chill. Cook the rice in vegetable stock or water, then drain well. Cook the spinach, fresh or frozen, until tender, drain thoroughly and chop coarsely. Cook the onion until soft but not brown in the oil, then add the spices and heat for a minute or two. Add the mushrooms, raise the heat a little and cook quickly, stirring often, until the mushrooms are tender and have released their juice. Mix the rice, spinach and mushroom mixture well together and season to taste with salt and a little pepper, then leave to cool. Assemble as above, but cut 'V' shapes out of the trimmings and arrange them in a chevron pattern along the length of the roll. Bake at a lower temperature – 190°C/375°F/Gas 5 for 30 minutes to cook the pastry and brown it nicely.

Serve huge bowls of mixed salad with the Immense Sausage Rolls.

Summer Puddings

1kg (2¼lb) mixed soft or softish
  fruit
225g (8oz) caster sugar
12 thin slices good quality white
  bread, crusts removed

Everyone has their own recipe for this traditional English pudding, so it is a good idea to mix the styles. I once had a Jamaican version made with papaya and pineapple in a rum-flavoured syrup which was tremendous and I now mix my fruit with much greater abandon. The basic recipe, of course, is as follows.

Cut two circles from slices of bread to fit in the bottoms of two 750ml (1½pt) pudding basins. Cut the remaining slices to line the sides of the basins, keeping back two slices to use as lids. Put the fruit into a heavy pan with the sugar and cook over a low heat until the juice starts to run. Spoon the fruit and its juice into the basins, fit on the bread lids, then place saucers or small plates which will just sit inside the top of the basins. Put something fairly heavy on top to weight the saucers down and leave the puddings in the fridge overnight. Next day turn them out on to pretty plates. If they look a little dry, or if the fruit you are using is not particularly juicy, cook some extra fruit and sugar into a thick syrup, strain and spoon over the turned-out puddings. Serve with whipped cream.

ANNUS
MIRABILIS

ANNUS MIRABILIS

Some years are particularly memorable, a whole twelve months of triumphs, some small and others of landmark size, but all adding up to a personal or family *annus mirabilis*. By his own admission, 1665 was Sir Isaac Newton's *annus mirabilis* – the year in which, among other discoveries, 'I began to think of gravity extending to the orb of the Moon'. This was during his time at *Woolsthorpe Manor*, the house where he was born, in a then remote hamlet in Lincolnshire that is now bordered by the A1. In 1665 he returned there to escape the plague in Cambridge, where he had just received his degree.

For Joshua Gee, the silk-merchant with colonial interests and friend of William Penn (one of the founders of Pennsylvania), 1707 must have been an *annus mirabilis*. He bought *Fenton House*, in Hampstead, and married a rich second wife (who presumably enabled him to purchase this desirable London – or rather village – property). Then, to crown his luck, this golden wife presented him with his first son and heir. Choosing a celebration menu for Gee's *annus mirabilis* is rendered rather difficult by his book *Trade and Navigation*, the subtitle of which is 'That the surest way for a Nation to increase in Riches, is to prevent the Importation of such Commodities as may be raised at Home'. However, the menu could include turtle soup, and a punch in which limes played a part, since neither turtle nor limes were produced at home. A pineapple might be on the menu, these having been grown in the gardens of any man of substance for the last 50 years. A dish of potato cakes, served as a sweet dish in the manner of the day might also have featured. Some of the recipes could have been Pennsylvanian – the corn soups of the early settlers, for instance. But whether corn would have been obtainable in London then is not known. I shall take gastronomic licence on that. This menu would also make a good Thanksgiving celebration.

Isaac Newton's year of good fortune could only be celebrated with an apple menu, ending with an Upside-down Apple Tart.

A Thanksgiving Dinner

Corn Soup
Braised Turkey with Celery Sauce
Mrs Glasse's Potato Cakes
An Evelyn Salad
Pineapple in Rum Syrup
Lime Sorbet

for eight

Corn Soup

350g (12oz) frozen sweet corn
100g (4oz) chopped celery,
    including some leaves
600ml (1pt) water
large handful parsley
1 bayleaf
600ml (1pt) milk
½ small onion, finely chopped
clove garlic, finely chopped
25g (1oz) butter
25g (1oz) flour
salt, freshly ground pepper
3 tablespoons single cream
pinch paprika
parsley, finely chopped,
    to garnish

This soup, loosely based on a Pennsylvanian recipe, is a more elegant version of the ubiquitous corn chowder which is thick enough to be a meal in itself. This recipe is equally good hot or cold.

Simmer the first five ingredients together, with a lid on the pan, for about 25 minutes, until the vegetables are soft. Meanwhile add the onion and the garlic to the milk and bring it slowly to the boil. Take it off the heat, cover the pan and leave it to infuse. Strain both the vegetable stock and the milk into a large jug; reserve 2–3 tablespoonfuls of the cooked sweet corn and celery mixture. Melt the butter in the soup pan, add the flour and stir well, then gradually add the corn stock and milk mixture. Stir continuously over a medium heat until the soup thickens a little and comes up to the boil. Check that the taste of raw flour has gone, and season generously with salt, freshly ground pepper and paprika. Add the cream and check the seasoning again. Whether you are eating this hot or cold, serve with a spoonful of the reserved corn in each bowl and sprinkled with a little parsley.

Braised Turkey with Celery Sauce

1 small (3·5kg, about 7lb)
 oven-ready turkey
1 large head celery
½ bottle medium dry white wine
50g (2oz) butter
4 tablespoons groundnut oil
bouquet garni (include a strip
 of lemon peel and plenty of
 parsley)

FOR THE STUFFING

225g (8oz) lean pork
225g (8oz) fat unsmoked bacon
50g (2oz) fresh breadcrumbs
1 large egg, beaten
large pinch grated nutmeg
small pinch ground cloves
salt and freshly ground pepper

TO FINISH THE SAUCE

25g (1oz) flour
25g (1oz) butter
150ml (¼pt) double cream

The turkey was established in England as early as 1540, then taken by settlers to New England. These domesticated fowls were ancestors to the inflated birds which are traditionally served at Christmas in Britain, and for Thanksgiving in the USA. The best treatment is to pick a small one and then braise, rather than roast it, partnering it with a vegetable purée rather than the ubiquitous brussel sprout. Hannah Glasse, like a number of her contemporaries, served a celery sauce with it which is delicious.

First make the stuffing. Mince or chop finely the two meats and mix with the breadcrumbs, egg and seasonings. Stuff the bird with this and close the cavity opening with metal skewers. Season the turkey outside with salt and pepper. Then, using a deep casserole, brown it slowly all over in the oil, which will take about 20 minutes. Heat the oven to 170°C/350°F/Gas 4. While the turkey is browning, prepare the celery. If it is the clean supermarket sort, you need only trim off the stale tops of the stalks and the elderly rootstump and simply slice across the whole head, leaves and all. Otherwise you will have to clean it thoroughly. Sauté the celery in a separate pan, in the butter with a sprinkling of salt. When the turkey is sufficiently brown, remove it and arrange some of the sautéd celery as a bed. Replace the bird breast down on this and then add the rest of the celery, the wine and the bouquet garni, plus a little more salt and pepper. Put foil over the casserole, then the lid and transfer to the oven for 1½ hours, or until the turkey's legs part easily from the carcase. Put the turkey on a warmed serving dish and keep it warm in a low oven while you finish the sauce. Discard the bouquet garni and tip the celery and its cooking juices into a blender or food processor and process to a smooth purée – you should have at least 750ml (1½pt). Melt the butter in a heavy pan and stir in the flour, then add the heated cream slowly and stir until you have a thick smooth sauce. Add the celery purée bit by bit until you have a fairly thick pouring sauce. Check the seasoning and pour into a warmed sauce boat.

Mrs Glasse's Potato Cakes

1·5kg (3lb) floury potatoes
2 egg yolks
2 tablespoons sherry
25g (1oz) butter
1 teaspoon soft brown sugar
pinch grated nutmeg
sunflower or groundnut oil

Quite the nicest potato dish with turkey, and labour-saving too as you can prepare them beforehand and leave the frying to the last minute.

Peel the potatoes, boil in lightly salted water, drain and mash them. While they are still hot, beat in the butter, egg yolks, sherry, sugar and nutmeg, then leave to get cold – overnight is best. Next day, shape into small cakes and roll in flour, then shallow-fry in hot oil until brown and crisp. Mrs Glasse suggests frying in butter, but they are crisper and lighter fried in oil.

An Evelyn Salad

John Evelyn, in his *A Discourse on Sallets*, published in 1699, praised the lettuce above all other plants and herbs as a salad ingredient. It is, he says, 'the principal Foundation of the universal Tribe of Sallets, which is to Cool and Refresh'. He would have been pleased at the numerous varieties available today. For this salad, after the richness of the braised turkey, serve a mixture of every available lettuce with a dressing made of orange juice instead of vinegar (another Evelyn suggestion) and a light olive oil.

Pineapple in Rum Syrup

1 large pineapple
225g (8oz) pale soft
   brown sugar
sherry glass rum
600ml (1pt) water
toasted flaked almonds

Make the syrup by dissolving the sugar in the water over a low heat and then simmering fast for 15 minutes. Cool a little, add the rum and allow to cool completely. Prepare the pineapple; cut off the tuft of leaves and reserve if they are in good condition. Peel the fruit and remove all the eyes with the tip of a potato peeler, then slice, core each slice and cut it into cubes – not too small. Mix with the syrup and keep at room temperature. Just before serving scatter the almonds on top and place the tuft of leaves in the centre. Serve with the Lime Sorbet.

Lime Sorbet

2 limes
2 egg whites
3 tablespoons lime marmalade
600ml (1pt) water
275g (10oz) caster sugar

Scrub the limes and remove their peel with a lemon zester, if you have one. If not, remove the peel very thinly with a potato peeler and cut it into very thin matchstick strips. Cover the peel with water and bring to the boil – simmer for 5 minutes, drain and cover with more water. Bring to the boil again and simmer for another 5 minutes. Drain and refresh in cold water, then drain well. Make a syrup with the water and sugar, boiling fast for 10 minutes after all the sugar has dissolved. Cool a little then add the lime marmalade and stir until smooth. Add the strained juice and peel of the limes and leave to cool completely. Tip into a shallow plastic box and freeze for 2–3 hours, stirring from time to time. Whisk the egg whites until billowy, then gradually add the semi-frozen syrup as you continue to whisk. When both are combined return to the freezer. Remove to the fridge 30 minutes before serving.

Brandy snaps filled with whipped cream flavoured with a little of the syrup from a jar of preserved ginger go perfectly with this combination of flavours.

Sir Isaac Newton's Apple Menu

Apple Salad with Smoked Meats
Chicken with Cider and Chestnuts
Cabbage with Apple
Upside-down Apple Tart

for four

Apple Salad with Smoked Meats

3 large Cox's or Kidd's Orange
Red apples
8 thin slices air-dried or
smoked meat
1 tablespoon lemon juice
6 tablespoons walnut oil
salt and freshly ground pepper
pinch allspice
freshly and finely chopped
celery leaves

There are few better ways to start a meal than with a sharp, appetite-whetting apple salad. Here it is partnered with a selection of smoked or cured meats – buy whatever is available. I like to use smoked venison and an air-dried ham from Dorset, called Denhay, but you could use Parma ham, or Spanish serrano ham, both of which are widely stocked.

First, make the dressing by combining the lemon juice, walnut oil, salt, pepper and allspice. Beat well with a whisk until they form a thick emulsion. Core the apples, cut them into dice and fold thoroughly into the dressing – do this quickly to stop the apple going brown. Arrange a portion of the apple on each plate and then place the meats around it. Sprinkle a little of the chopped celery leaves on the apple as a garnish, and serve with warm granary rolls.

Chicken with Cider and Chestnuts

1 x 2kg (4lb) free-range or
maize-fed chicken
225g (8oz) ready-prepared
chestnuts
4 rashers unsmoked streaky
bacon
600ml (1pt) dry cider
3–4 tablespoons groundnut oil
1 tablespoon coarse ground
mustard
3–4 tablespoons crème fraîche
salt and freshly ground pepper
seasoned flour
bouquet garni

Joint the chicken, divide the leg pieces and each side of the breast into two, and dust with seasoned flour. Cut the bacon into strips and brown it in the hot oil, remove with a draining spoon and reserve. Brown the chicken pieces on both sides in the same oil. Place both chicken and bacon pieces in a casserole. Bring the cider to the boil and pour it over, add the bouquet garni and a little salt and pepper (bearing in mind both the seasoned flour and the bacon), cover and simmer gently for about 35 minutes, or until the chicken is tender. Remove the chicken and place on a serving dish to keep warm while you make the sauce. Discard the bouquet garni and add the chestnuts to the cider sauce in which the chicken cooked. Simmer steadily, in the open pan, for about 10 minutes to reduce the liquid and concentrate the flavour. Add the crème fraîche and the mustard and stir well, check the seasoning and pour over the waiting chicken pieces. Serve with a decorative dusting of finely chopped parsley, new potatoes boiled in their skins and the cabbage.

Cabbage with Apple

about 685g (1½lb) finely shredded Savoy cabbage
1 small cooking apple, peeled, cored and sliced
85ml (3fl oz) hot chicken stock
2 cloves garlic, peeled
40g (1½oz) butter
salt and freshly grated nutmeg

Red cabbage cooked with apple in the German fashion has become an English favourite, too, but I like Savoy cabbage cooked in the same way even better and it is a good-tempered vegetable dish which will look after itself.

Melt the butter over a low heat and cook the apple slices in it, stirring to prevent them catching. When they have softened a little, add the cabbage. Toss it with the butter and apple so that all the shreds are well mixed and cook very gently for 5 minutes. Tip all into an ovenproof dish with a well-fitting lid, bury the two garlic cloves in the centre, add the hot stock and the seasoning (go easy on the nutmeg – you only want a suspicion), cover and cook for about 45 minutes in a low oven (160°C/325°F/Gas 3). Check that the casserole neither dries out nor cooks too slowly – this is *not* meant to be served *al dente*. Just before serving, when the apples and the garlic have cooked to a melted softness, stir the contents of the dish with a wooden fork to mix all together without breaking up the cabbage.

Upside-down Apple Tart

225g (8oz) sweet shortcrust pastry (see page 32)

FOR THE FILLING
685g (1½lb) approx. well-flavoured English eating apples
6 tablespoons quince jelly
squeeze lemon juice
2 tablespoons pale soft brown sugar
knob unsalted butter

This is an anglicised version of Tarte Tatin. It is much easier to turn out and although it does not look quite as elegant as the French version, tastes wonderful. This recipe also has a faint flavour of quince, which legend maintains was Isaac Newton's favourite fruit. If you are fed up with apples by now, use pears, or quinces on their own.

Butter a non-stick 22cm (9in) cake tin. Roll out the pastry reasonably thinly and cut out a circle to fit the cake tin. Chill this circle in the fridge. Peel, core and slice the apples, then melt the butter in a heavy saucepan and add the sugar. Cook over a medium heat until the sugar begins to caramelise; when it is uniformly brown and bubbling take it off the heat (left any longer, it will burn) and add the quince jelly, stirring all the time so that it melts with the caramel. Add the apple slices and return to a medium heat, stirring gently to

cover the slices with the syrup. Cook for about 6–7 minutes, until the slices are soft, but not slushy. Add a squeeze of lemon juice to sharpen the flavour, then transfer to the cake tin. Heat the oven to 200°C/400°F/Gas 6. Place the pastry circle on top of the apples and bake for about 12–15 minutes, until the pastry is cooked and beginning to colour. Place a plate, upside-down, over the cake tin and swiftly turn the whole thing over, so that the pastry arrives safely on the plate, with the apples neatly on the pastry. If, despite the buttering of the cake tin, a few bits of apple stick, just scrape them off and add them to the rest, and if the apples have not arrived all that neatly on the pastry base, just tidy them up before serving. If you have it, a spoonful or two of calvados or English apple brandy poured over the apples just before serving improves the flavour even more. Serve warm, with plenty of chilled double cream.

THEATRICAL
SUCCESSES

THEATRICAL SUCCESSES

Theatrical entertainment has always been popular in country houses, whether in the form of amateur efforts or a visit from more professional talent. In the sixteenth and seventeenth centuries such entertainment was often accompanied or followed by 'banqueting stuff', a succession of light snacks in the form of sweetmeats. These sweetmeats might follow a formal meal, too, a practice represented today by the chocolates or petit fours served with coffee.

In the early seventeenth century, Richard Shuttleworth of *Gawthorpe Hall*, Lancashire, was an enthusiastic patron of the performing arts, engaging troupes of players on a regular basis and often paying them considerable sums. At that time Gawthorpe guests are likely to have been offered gilded sweetmeats made of almond paste and flavoured with rosewater as post-theatrical snacks.

The 5th Marquess of Anglesey, something of an eccentric, converted the chapel at *Plas Newydd*, on Anglesey, into a theatre in the early 1900s. Here he staged elaborate productions which probably helped, eventually, to bankrupt him, especially as he hired the services of several noted London actors and actresses to eke out his own talent, although he often took the leading role.

Amateur theatricals were very much to the taste of Crown Prince Vajiravudh of Siam while he was staying with the Colchester-Wemyss family at *Westbury Court*, in Gloucestershire, at the beginning of this century. The Crown Prince, under the pen name of Carlton H. Terris, wrote three short comedies in which he and members of his suite took the main roles. The evening's entertainment was lavishly provided with the very best of sets and costumes and even souvenir programmes, and supper was served in a marquee after the performance.

On a more professional note, Sybil Thorndyke and Lewis Casson were frequent visitors to *Wallington*, Northumberland, when playing in Newcastle. Mrs John Dower, daughter of Sir Charles Trevelyan, was brought up at Wallington and remembers waiting up for them and then retiring 'to the kitchen for a great party round the kitchen table with the cook's beautiful brown buns and soup'.

We can still be entertained at country houses and stately homes – 'events' staged at many Trust houses fill the summer months. Depending on the weather and distance, catering for such an evening can mean eating before you set out and

rounding off with a 'Wallington supper' on your return, or taking a picnic which can be divided into stages to fit in with the intervals. For this kind of staged eating, something like Hannah's Glasse's 'Salamongundy' or salmagundi, is ideal. I have not given a specific recipe for it, as it is a combination of all your favourite salad ingredients, either arranged in small dishes around a large platter, or all arranged together in a pyramid – which tends to look a wreck very quickly once everyone has helped themselves. You can use combinations of chicken, strips of roast beef, ham (cooked, air-dried or smoked), salt fish such as anchovies, smoked salmon, even smoked haddock which is delicious raw if you use the undyed sort, and hard-boiled eggs. Use raw, cooked or pickled vegetables, any of the wide variety of salad leaves, and crown everything with edible flowers, especially nasturtium, bergamot and borage. Either use a vinaigrette to season the ingredients, or, better still, offer it separately.

If the entertainment is indoors in the winter, a light supper afterwards is ideal if your cooker has an automatic timer. While I am not suggesting you serve jugged hare or roast lamb so late at night, the smell of a Parmesan-topped pasta dish turning golden in the oven as you open the front door is the height of welcoming hospitality.

Summer Buffet for a Crown Prince

The Colchester-Wemyss Prawn and Cucumber Curry
The Colchester-Wemyss Avocado Salad
Coconut Fried Rice
Vegetables with Lime Dressing
Mango and Papaya Compote

for six

This menu is as good cold as hot, so it doubles as a picnic for theatrical events. The first two recipes are adapted from *The Pleasures of the Table* by Sir Francis Colchester-Wemyss, published in 1931. Sir Francis gained his culinary knowledge as mess secretary to his regiment while serving in India, and applied this to English cooks in a fashion which might not always have found favour with them (he recommended

a weekly 'kit inspection' of pots and pans). His recipes are excellent, however, and while not exactly what his relations served to the Crown Prince of Siam, do have a similar gamut of flavours, mild and fragrant rather than hot. This curry, which he calls a 'typical good-class dish', is an excellent example.

The Colchester-Wemyss Prawn and Cucumber Curry

1 large cucumber
685g (1½lb) frozen prawns
1 large mild onion
2 tablespoons groundnut
 or sunflower oil
50g (2oz) creamed coconut
450ml (¾pt) hot water
450ml (¾pt) hot fish stock
2 tablespoons flour
2 tablespoons finely chopped
 fresh ginger
1½ teaspoons turmeric
2 pinches grated nutmeg
1 large bayleaf
salt
fresh lemon juice
finely chopped fresh coriander
crème fraîche or yoghourt –
 see method

Peel the cucumber and cut it lengthways into four, then cut across at roughly 1·5cm (¾in) intervals to make large chunks. Add these to a pan of boiling salted water, bring the water back to the boil and cook for 2 minutes. Drain thoroughly. Thaw the prawns by spreading them in a single layer on a thick mattress of kitchen paper to absorb the liquid as they defrost. Slice the onion finely and cook until pale gold and soft in the oil, together with the ginger, turmeric and nutmeg. Dissolve the coconut in the hot water. When the onion is soft add the flour, off the heat, then add the hot coconut water and the fish stock, stirring until all has amalgamated and there are no floury lumps. Add the bayleaf, bring to the boil, stirring well, and simmer fast for about 15 minutes. Add the prawns and cucumber and bring back to a fast simmer, but as soon as it begins to bubble, draw off the heat, cover tightly and leave for another 15 minutes. Taste and add more salt if the fish stock and prawns have not added enough and a teaspoon or two of lemon juice. Garnish with chopped coriander. Reheat, or keep warm, in a bowl over a pan of very hot water rather than direct heat, which toughens the prawns.

If serving cold, thicken the sauce a little with crème fraîche or yoghourt.

The Colchester-Wemyss Avocado Salad

Sir Francis was breaking new ground with this tropical dish in the 1930s, and quite rightly says 'there is something extraordinarily attractive about this exotic salad'. Even now, when the avocado has become something of a cliché, it can

be delicious if prepared imaginatively and in this menu acts as a relish rather than a salad.

Allow half a ripe avocado per person and make a vinaigrette using lemon juice, and add plenty of freshly ground black pepper. Instead of pouring the vinaigrette into the well left by the stone, scoop the flesh away from the skin with a teaspoon and mix well with the vinaigrette, then serve in the skins. This has the added advantage that the lemon juice prevents the flesh from discolouring.

Coconut Fried Rice

275g (10oz) basmati rice
water – see method
50g (2oz) desiccated coconut
1 fresh chilli
3 cardamom pods
salt
groundnut or sunflower oil
toasted coconut flakes, from
    health food stores – (optional)

For this you need delicious, expensive basmati rice – no other will do.

Measure the rice as you weigh it, using a cup or mug, then measure exactly double the amount of water and set this aside. Soak the rice in salted water for about 20 minutes, then drain. Heat 2 tablespoonfuls of oil and add the bruised cardamom pods and the chilli, with its seeds removed. Stir in the oil for about a minute, then add the drained rice and the coconut, stirring all well together so that the oil coats every grain of rice. Add the water you have set aside and a teaspoonful of salt and bring to the boil. Boil fairly fast until the water has evaporated and the surface of the rice is pitted with little holes. Place a folded tea towel over the pan, put the lid on top and leave, on the lowest possible heat, for 15 minutes. Bite a grain of rice to check if it is cooked. If it is not, replace the cloth and lid and leave for another 5 minutes. All the water will have been absorbed. Fluff up the rice with a wooden fork and spread it on a dish to cool a little. Heat a thin film of oil in a large frying pan and add the rice, then stir-fry over a high heat for about 8 minutes, or until the rice is beginning to crisp and is dry and crumbly. Garnish with the toasted coconut flakes. Either serve this hot (in which case leave the frying as a reheating measure) or cold.

Vegetables with Lime Dresssing

685g (1½lb) prepared seasonal
vegetables – broccoli, red and
yellow peppers, celery, french
beans, mange-touts, baby
sweet corn, courgettes
4 tablespoons olive oil
juice 1 lime
2 tablespoons light soy sauce
2 tablespoons sesame seeds
1 tablespoon runny honey
freshly ground black pepper

This is a crunchy, aromatic vegetable dish, satisfying hot or cold and good enough on its own, partnered with the rice and the avocado, to make a meal for vegetarians who do not want the prawn curry.

Make sure the vegetables are in small pieces of roughly the same size – carrots, courgettes and celery cut into thick matchsticks, the broccoli broken into small florets, the peppers finely sliced, and so on. In a jam jar, shake together the lime juice, honey and soy sauce. Heat the olive oil in a large frying pan or, better still, a wok, and stir-fry the vegetables for 6–7 minutes, adding the sesame seeds during the last minute. Tip into a shallow dish and mix immediately, while they are still warm, with the dressing and season with plenty of freshly ground black pepper – the soy provides the salt.

After all these aromatic flavours, a combination of ripe papaya and mango in an orange-flower scented syrup is very soothing.

Mango and Papaya Compote

2 ripe papayas (they should be
yellowish, rather than green)
2 ripe mangoes
syrup (see page 74)
orange flower water
juice 1 orange

Make up the syrup as on page 74, but flavour it with about 2 teaspoons (or to taste) of orange flower water instead of the rum, and add the juice of the orange off the heat. Leave this to cool completely while you prepare the fruit. Halve the papayas and scoop out the dramatic black seeds; peel the halves then cut the flesh in long slices. Slice the mango flesh away from the stone, then peel each piece and dice the flesh. Mix the two fruits with the syrup and leave in a cold place until ready to serve.

A Kitchen Supper

Leek, Mussel and Bacon Soup
Potted Trout and Oatcakes
Blackberry and Apple Pancakes

for eight

This is a cosy informal meal, perhaps more suitable for the kitchen at Wallington than the Crown Prince's marquee.

Leek, Mussel and Bacon Soup

1kg (2lb) mussels in their shells
4 leeks, trimmed of their green leaves and finely sliced
2 large red-skinned potatoes, peeled and cubed
4 rashers unsmoked middle-back bacon, snipped into strips
600ml (1pt) creamy milk
850ml (1½pt) water
salt and freshly ground black pepper
1 small onion, sliced
1 bayleaf
pinch mace
finely chopped parsley

This is a chunky soup-stew, filling enough to serve before the play or concert and to keep appetites at bay until the interval.

Scrub the mussels under a running tap, and discard any which are open and do not close immediately you give them a sharp tap. Remove the 'beards'. Bring 300ml (½pt) of water to the boil in a large pan, tip in the mussels, put the lid on and return to a high heat. Boil briskly, shaking the pan, for about 5 minutes, then check that all the shells have opened. If not, stir the contents with a wooden fork and return to the boil and continue for another minute or so. Strain the liquid through a sieve lined with a piece of muslin or a new J-cloth into a measuring jug, and, when they are cool enough to handle, extract the mussels from their shells and reserve.

In another, heavy, pan, cook the bacon until its fat begins to run. If it does not, because it is the sort which merely oozes salty liquid, add a thread of oil to help it out. As the bacon frizzles, add the sliced leeks and potatoes and a sprinkling of salt. Mix well, lower the heat, put a lid on the pan and cook gently for 10 minutes. Add the strained shellfish liquor, plus enough water to cover the vegetables by about an inch, and simmer gently until the vegetables are almost cooked. Meanwhile, heat the milk with the sliced onion and bayleaf until it is just about to boil, draw it off the heat and leave it to

infuse while the vegetables cook. Add the strained milk to the vegetables, together with the mussels. Season with salt, pepper and mace and reheat until thoroughly hot, but do not boil. Garnish with finely chopped parsley and serve with brown bread or rolls and lots of salty butter.

Potted Trout and Oatcakes

3 whole trout, gutted
thyme
1 lemon, sliced
salt and pepper
sunflower oil
about 175–225g (6–8oz)
*   butter*
lemon juice
mace or nutmeg

Heat the oven to 160°C/325°F/Gas 3. Season the trout inside and out with salt and pepper. Put a sheet of foil on a baking sheet, and brush the foil lightly with oil. Sprinkle the oiled foil with thyme and place three lemon slices on it, then place a trout on each lemon slice. Sprinkle the fish with more thyme and arrange the remaining lemon slices on top. Cover with another sheet of oiled foil, pinching both sheets together to make a neat, loose package. Bake the trout for 25 minutes in the centre of the oven, then remove the top sheet of foil and allow the fish to cool. When they are cool enough to handle, remove all skin and bones and flake the flesh. Weigh it, and put it in a food processor or blender, plus half its weight in soft butter. Process until smooth, then season with salt and mace or nutmeg and a squeeze or two of lemon juice. Turn into a deep dish and melt a little more butter to pour over the surface. Refrigerate until needed, but take it out of the fridge about 30 minutes before eating (while you are serving the soup), to allow the flavours to develop. Serve with crisp, warmed oatcakes and lemon wedges.

Blackberry and Apple Pancakes

FOR THE PANCAKE BATTER

300ml (½pt) skimmed milk
100g (4oz) flour
2 eggs
1 tablespoon vanilla sugar
25g (1oz) melted unsalted butter
sunflower oil for frying

FOR THE FILLING

225g (8oz) blackberries
1 large cooking apple
4 dessert apples
50g (2oz) unsalted butter
100g (4oz) honey
1 teaspoon cinnamon
6 tablespoons orange juice, or calvados
demerara sugar

Makes twelve pancakes

Make both pancakes and their filling a day or two before and store in the fridge – or even weeks before and freeze them. Assemble them before you go out and heat them in the oven while you are eating the first two courses.

To make the batter, put the first four ingredients into a food processor or blender, and mix for about 30 seconds, or until smooth. Leave to stand for at least an hour. Blend again, this time adding the melted butter. Heat a small, heavy frying pan. Dip a small pad of kitchen paper in sunflower oil and wipe it swiftly round the inside of the hot pan. Add a ladleful of batter, tipping it so that it covers the base of the pan in a thin layer. When this has set and the surface is covered in tiny bubbles, loosen the pancake with a palette knife and flip it over, shaking the pan so that it settles smoothly in place. Cook another 30 seconds and turn it out on to a waiting plate. Continue in the same way until you have used up all the batter, wiping the pan every so often with oily paper, and stacking the pancakes on the plate. When they are quite cold, cover with foil and refrigerate or freeze.

To make the filling, peel, core and slice the apples. Melt the butter in a large frying pan, add the cinnamon and honey, heat until the honey has melted, then add the apple slices and toss them in this mixture, over a medium heat, until they are tender and slightly caramelised. Reduce the heat and add the blackberries, cooking gently until these, too, are tender, which takes about 5 minutes. Leave to cool. Place a couple of tablespoonfuls of the fruit mixture in the centre of each pancake and roll up. Arrange in a shallow baking dish, spoon over the orange juice or calvados (or a mixture), sprinkle thickly with demerara sugar and bake for about 25 minutes in the centre of a 190°C/375°F/Gas 5 oven. Serve with thick cream or Greek yoghourt.

Twentieth-century 'Banqueting Stuff'

Filled Rolls
Crudités and Dips
Apricot Creams
Walnut Tartlets
Iced Cheese

The great advantage of assembling a number of inconsequential mouthfuls, instead of one or two more substantial dishes, is that your guests can eat them before the performance, in the intervals or as a final flourish before setting off for home. Most of these can be prepared well in advance, will need the minimum of attention and are just right for taking to open-air performances.

Filled Rolls

Even if these remind you of railway buffets, read on. Hollowed-out rolls are brushed with olive oil, baked until crisp and then filled. These are the modern equivalent of the vol-au-vent, or the 'patties' so beloved of Victorian and Edwardian cooks, but these are much lighter as the fillings are not cemented with béchamel sauce.

Allow 1 large or 2 small roll(s) per person. I like to use miniature brown loaves, but any crusty roll will do and offering both brown and white is a good idea.

Heat the oven to 200°C/400°F/Gas 6. Remove a slice from the top of each roll and scoop out the crumb from inside, leaving a hollowed-out crust. Brush the inside with a light olive or groundnut oil, sprinkle sparingly with salt and place on a baking sheet. Bake for about 15 minutes, until the rolls are crisp but not overbrowned. Cool on a wire rack. Fill with any of the following fillings.

PARMA HAM AND MUSHROOM FILLING

6 large brown rolls

FOR THE FILLING

*350g (12oz) chestnut or
 brown cap mushrooms*
*4 slices Parma, or other
 air-dried ham, cut into
 thin strips*
4 tablespoons olive oil
1 teaspoon tomato purée
1 bayleaf
8 tablespoons warm water
1 crushed clove garlic
salt and pepper
finely chopped chives

Wipe and slice the mushrooms. Warm the olive oil gently in a frying pan and add the mushrooms and garlic. Cook over a low heat for about 5 minutes, then add the tomato purée mixed with the water, the bayleaf, salt and freshly ground pepper. Stir well to amalgamate all the ingredients and cook at a gentle simmer for another 5 minutes, until the mushrooms are just tender. Remove the mushrooms with a slotted spoon. Mix the strips of ham with the mushrooms and allow to get cold. Add the chives and spoon into the rolls.

GREEK SALAD FILLING

6 large white rolls

FOR THE FILLING

175g (6oz) feta cheese
12 cherry tomatoes, quartered
1 small cucumber
red wine vinegar
5 tablespoons olive oil
1 bruised clove garlic
fresh basil
salt and pepper

Peel strips off the cucumber to make it look striped, then dice it finely. Put it in a colander with a sprinkling of salt and leave it to drain for about 30 minutes. Meanwhile make the dressing so that the flavours can infuse. Put the olive oil, a few drops only of vinegar, a little salt, plenty of pepper and the bruised garlic into a jam-jar. Add as many basil leaves as you like, torn up but not chopped (the flavour of torn leaves is so much nicer than that of chopped). Put the lid on the jar, shake hard, then leave to stand. Crumble the cheese and put in a bowl with the tomatoes and drained cucumber, then add the dressing, removing the garlic. Toss the salad and fill the rolls.

90

MARINATED SALMON AND PRAWN FILLING

6 small brown rolls

FOR THE FILLING

350g (12oz) salmon tail,
  skinned and filleted
juice of 1 lime
2 teaspoons coarse sea salt
1 teaspoon crushed green
  peppercorns
1 finely chopped shallot
1 tablespoon finely chopped
  tarragon leaves
175g (6oz) frozen prawns
2 tablespoons light olive or
  sunflower oil
another tablespoon chopped
  tarragon
2–3 tablespoons Greek
  yoghourt

This must be made at least 24 hours ahead so the salmon can 'cure' in the marinade.

Check the fish minutely for any bones, then cut it into 1cm ($\frac{1}{2}$in) cubes. Mix together the lime juice, salt, peppercorns, shallot and tarragon and toss the salmon cubes in this, making sure they are well coated with the marinade. Place in a shallow dish, cover with foil and leave to marinate in the fridge for 24–36 hours, turning once or twice. When ready to assemble, thaw the prawns on paper towels so that they are not too wet, then mix with the drained salmon (reserve the marinade), the second tablespoonful of tarragon, the yoghourt and a little of the strained marinade to season. Fill the rolls.

GREEN VEGETABLE FILLING

6 small white rolls

FOR THE FILLING

225g (8oz) french beans, topped
  and tailed
175g (6oz) mange-touts, topped
  and tailed
2 courgettes, diced
175g (6oz) shelled green peas,
  fresh or frozen or 175g (6oz)
  shelled small broad beans,
  fresh or frozen
finely chopped chervil, parsley
  and chives
vinaigrette seasoned with coarse
  ground mustard

Cut the beans and mange-touts into 1cm ($\frac{1}{2}$in) lengths, and blanch or steam the vegetables until just cooked. While they are still warm, toss in the vinaigrette with the chopped herbs. Fill the rolls. You can use any mixture of vegetables, of course, but the fresh green colours in the white rolls looks particularly attractive and appetising, especially if you arrange them with the salmon filled rolls on the same platter.

Crudités and Dips

A saladophile like John Evelyn would have loved the idea of crudités, but he might have preferred a more interesting selection than the ubiquitous trio of carrots, celery and cauliflower. Try a selection of:

Little Gem lettuce hearts – cut into quarters or eighths
fennel bulbs – cut into eighths
corn-cobs – tiny and left whole
courgettes – sliced into batons
mushrooms – tiny button, raw and impaled on cocktail sticks
Belgian chicory – separated red and white leaves
carrots – raw, whole baby ones
peas – sugar snap or manges-tout, blanched briefly
beetroot – raw and cut into batons (an unjustly neglected treat)

These three dips are quick and easy to prepare.

CONSOMMÉ CURRY DIP

1 tin condensed consommé
225g (8oz) cream cheese
1 teaspoon medium hot curry paste
squeeze lemon juice
salt to taste
mayonnaise – see method

Put all the ingredients in the blender or processor and whiz together. For vegetarians, omit the consommé and add another teaspoon of curry paste plus three tablespoons of mayonnaise.

PINK FISH DIP

225g (8oz) cream cheese
3 tablespoons taramasalata
jar red lumpfish roe
1 teaspoon Spanish paprika
few drops Tabasco

Blend all ingredients together, except the lumpfish roe. Stir this into the blended sauce so that the tiny beads do not lose their identity or texture.

AVOCADO DIP

2 very ripe avocados
small tub plain yoghourt
cayenne
salt
finely chopped chives
lemon juice

Put the flesh of the avocados in the processor with the yoghourt, lemon juice and seasoning. Blend until smooth, then check the seasoning and stir in enough chopped chives to give a good but not overpowering flavour.

Apricot Creams

500g (1lb) dried apricots,
    soaked in 300ml ($\frac{1}{2}$pt) water
100g (4oz) runny honey
2 tablespoons madeira, apricot
    brandy or medium dry sherry
300ml ($\frac{1}{2}$pt) whipping cream
150ml ($\frac{1}{4}$pt) crème fraîche
toasted flaked almonds

Fills eight individual ramekins.
The strong flavour of dried apricots is underlined by the honey and then softened by the cream. It is best to use 'naturally' dried fruit, as that has the most flavour. Naturally dried apricots can be bought in good health food stores.

Cook the apricots in their soaking water until quite soft. Drain, then purée them in a food processor or blender, together with the honey (warm this if necessary to make it blend better) and your chosen alcohol. Whip the creams together and fold them in, then pour into individual ramekins or custard cups. Decorate with a few toasted flaked almonds.

Walnut Tartlets

FOR THE PASTRY

375g (12oz) plain flour
175g (6oz) butter
1 dessertspoon vanilla sugar
cold milk to mix

FOR THE FILLING

2 eggs
175g (6oz) vanilla sugar
75g (3oz) chopped walnuts
50g (2oz) currants
25g (1oz) chopped dates
25g (1oz) unsalted butter,
    melted
2 drops vanilla extract

Makes twenty-four tartlets.
These crisp nutty tartlets with their faint flavour of vanilla partner the dried apricot creams very well.

To make the pastry, mix the sugar and flour together then rub in the butter until fine. Add enough cold milk to mix, kneading the pastry into a smooth ball. Wrap in foil and chill for an hour. Heat the oven to 175°C/350°F/Gas 4. Roll out the pastry thinly and cut into circles using a large biscuit cutter. Use these circles to line greased bun tins. Put the tins in the fridge while you make the filling. Beat the eggs and sugar together in a bowl standing over a pan of hot water, until the mixture is thick and pale and the beaters leave a trail on the surface. Take off the hot water and fold in all the other ingredients very quickly and thoroughly. Put a large

teaspoonful into each pastry case, but do not be too generous as the filling rises and might overflow. Bake for about 25–30 minutes or until the filling is firm and the colour of a macaroon. These keep well in an air-tight tin so can be made in advance.

Iced Cheese

275g (10oz) cheese (see right), grated or crumbled
85g (3oz) cream cheese
3 tablespoons double cream
about 50g (2oz) medium oatmeal

This is rich, delicious and refreshing, but do not use a subtle cheese. The strong blue cheeses work best, or a very mature Cheddar of the type my grandmother used to call 'gum-tickling'.

Spread the oatmeal on a baking sheet and toast it under the grill or in a hot oven, until it is a golden brown (it burns easily), then leave it to get cold. In a food processor blend the cheeses and cream until smooth, then chill in the fridge for at least 3 hours. When it is quite firm, mould the cheese into a neat cylinder and roll it in the oatmeal until evenly coated. Wrap in greaseproof paper and then cling film and chill until ready to serve. If you are taking this on a picnic, keep it in the freezer until you leave, then it will defrost to just the right temperature by the time you get to the end of the meal. Serve with crisp biscuits and celery or grapes.

ROYAL
PROGRESS

ROYAL PROGRESS

One of the hazards (or perhaps one of the aims) of having built yourself a fine country house was that inevitably a peripatetic member of the royal family would invite themselves to stay. This meant equipping a number of state rooms, including a bedroom complete with bed hung with ruinously expensive hangings. Such beds can be seen at *Erddig*, in Clwyd, and *Kedleston* in Derbyshire.

It also meant much feasting and celebrating, inviting the county to bask in your reflected glory. In some cases, as Prince Pückler-Muskau wrote to his wife during his long visit to England from 1826 to 1829, the lavish display the English put on for visitors to their country houses, royal or otherwise, was not kept up after the visitors had departed, 'many a family atones for it by meagre fare when alone; for which reason nobody here ventures to pay a visit in the country without first being invited'. This was probably true, if one reads between the rather rueful lines written by Miss Iremonger after she and her aunt, Lady Fetherstonhaugh, had to depart 'from *Uppark* [Sussex] to vacate our places to the Prince and his Party . . . . Three Hot made Dishes of meat were to form a regular part of each morning's breakfast if the Duc de Chartres came . . . .' The Prince of Wales (later George IV) was a frequent visitor to Uppark in the 1780s, enjoying the racing on West Harting Down. Lady Fetherstonhaugh lists the supplies 'for upward of 80 in the family . . . 3 days entertainment in Aug 1784 for the Prince of Wales, 12 in company . . . . 2 Bucks, a Welsh sheep, a doz. Ducks 4 Hams, dozens of Pigeons, and Rabbits, Flitches of Bacon, Lobsters and Prawns; a Turtle of 120lbs; 166lbs butter, 376 Eggs, 67 Chickens, 23 Pints of Cream, 30lbs of Coffee, 10lbs of Fine Tea; and 3lbs of common tea.' To transform such provisions into dishes fit for a prince, Sir Harry Fetherstonhaugh could boast a notable French chef, Moget, to match the skills of Prinny's own chef, Antonin Carême, at his extraordinary Pavilion in nearby Brighthelmstone (Brighton).

In 1619, when the Prince of Wales, later to be Charles I, dined with the Earl of Devonshire at *Hardwick Hall* in Derbyshire, fifteen cooks and 'John Burtram the London Cook' were hired to provide a suitably opulent repast. It seems to have been necessary to buy in food from the neighbours, too, including poultry and fish, half a stag and a calf, cheeses, apples and apricots. Towards the end of that century, William III, visiting *Belton House* in Lincolnshire, was so amply wined and dined by

his host Sir John Brownlow, '12 fat oxen and 60 sheep besides other victuals for his entertainment', noted the diarist de la Pryme, that on proceeding to Lincoln, he was able to 'eat nothing but a mess of milk'.

George III made a royal progress through the West Country in 1789, dropping in at *Saltram*, near Plymouth, and subsequently ennobling his delightfully gregarious host, John Parker, as a reward for the comfort and elegance he had obviously enjoyed. Then, with Queen Charlotte, he visited nearby *Cotehele*, in Cornwall, travelling up the River Tamar in the private barge of John Parker (now Lord Boringdon). The party enjoyed some light refreshment before returning the same way to Saltram. Henry Sharington of *Lacock Abbey*, Wiltshire, got off lightly; Queen Elizabeth bestowed a knighthood on him for a single meal under his roof.

At *Cragside*, in Northumberland, the stream of royalty, often coming from abroad to buy arms from William Armstrong for their respective countries, seems to have been never-ending. In 1889 the local paper noted a particularly plucky attempt to offer the Shah of Persia his native food at the banquet held in his honour: 'Two or three Persian dishes were served – notably pilau, an arrangement of chicken with rice boiled in stock. . . . A peculiar feature of the repast was several small dishes of pickles placed in the immediate vicinity of the Shah, who, we understand, is very fond of picking up a pickle with his fingers and eating it as a relish to his dinner.'

A dinner in the classical haute-Edwardian style was held at *Mount Stewart* in County Down during the visit of King Edward VII and Queen Alexandra in 1903. Course after course, beginning with the inevitable turtle soup and ending with a savoury, was set before their majesties. Much simpler, and probably rather more welcome, was the admirably brief menu for lunch offered to Queen Elizabeth (the present Queen Mother) at *Lanhydrock* in Cornwall on 11 July 1950 – salmon trout (a speciality of the house, caught in the Fowey), served with a green sauce, then poulet au riz (the forerunner of Coronation Chicken, invented for her daughter's coronation only three years later), and finally a raspberry mousse.

The Shah's Banquet

Lamb Pilau
Munkaczina
Chilled Walnut and Prune Compote
Spiced Almond Shortcakes

for eight

This banquet has all the flavours of 'The Arabian Nights', as Mrs Leyel noted in her chapter of such recipes in her book *The Gentle Art of Cookery* (1936). The recipe for Munkaczina, a refreshing and unusual salad, is from the book.

Lamb Pilau

1·5kg (3lb) boned shoulder
   of lamb
large bunch thyme
cinnamon stick
1 mild onion, sliced
85g (3oz) pistachio nuts
2 tablespoons dried cherries
   or raisins
550g (1¼lb) basmati rice
olive oil
salt
allspice

Cut the lamb into cubes about 1cm (½in) square and put them in a heavy pan with the thyme, cinnamon stick and onion, then add 1.75 litres (3 pints) water and a teaspoon of salt and bring slowly to the boil. Skim any froth that rises to the surface, then lower the heat, cover the pan and simmer for 40 minutes. While the meat is cooking, weigh the rice and measure its volume, then rinse it well and leave it to soak in a bowl of cold water. Strain the stock from the lamb and remove the thyme and cinnamon stick. Measure into a large jug twice the volume of stock as that of the rice (ie 2 cups of rice to 4 cups of stock). Pour a thin film of oil into a heavy casserole, warm it gently and add the drained rice, stirring it well so that each grain is coated with oil. Pour in the hot stock and add the cherries or raisins. Simmer fast, uncovered, until the surface is pitted with little holes. Arrange the meat and onion on the rice, with the pistachio nuts, and cover with a doubled tea towel, then the lid of the casserole. Leave to cook, on the lowest possible heat or in a very low oven (140°C/275°F/Gas 1) for another 25 minutes. Remove the lid and cloth and fork the rice and meat together, seasoning with a little more salt and a pinch of allspice.

Munkaczina (Orange and onion salad)

4 large navel oranges
½ large mild Spanish onion
*   or 1 red onion*
175g (6oz) stoned black olives
2 teaspoons mild paprika
pinch cayenne
salt
3 tablespoons olive oil
finely chopped parsley

Munkaczina, claimed Mrs Leyel, was 'brought from the East by Anatole France'. She does not specify what sort of onion should be used, but I find red, or mild Spanish, onions are best. The salad goes well with the pilaff.

Peel the oranges thickly, taking off all the pith. Slice them horizontally and remove the little plug of pith from the centre of each slice. Arrange the slices over the base of a shallow dish. Chop the peeled onion finely and spread it on top of the orange slices, leaving a clear border of orange, then slice the olives and spread them over the onion. Sprinkle with the paprika, cayenne and a little salt, then dribble the olive oil over the top. Some finely chopped parsley adds another dash of colour to the sophisticated orange and black colour scheme.

Chilled Walnut and Prune Compote

675g (1½lb) prunes d'Agen
900ml (1½pt) freshly brewed,
*   infused and strained Earl Grey*
*   or jasmine tea*
225g (8oz) shelled walnuts
honey to taste
cinnamon stick
wineglassful medium dry sherry

For this recipe you need the best prunes, and the very best are the prunes d'Agen sold by Marks & Spencer and good food shops.

The prunes should not need soaking. Put them and the cinnamon stick to cook in the tea, which should cover them by about 2·5cm (1in), add water if necessary. While they cook, which will take about 20 minutes' gentle simmering, cover the walnuts with cold water, bring to the boil, boil for about 30 seconds and drain. Cover with fresh water and repeat the process, then drain and set aside. Remove as much of the brown skin as you can, but as the double blanching process has removed much of the bitterness from the skin, you need not be too fussy. When the prunes are tender, lift them from the cooking liquid with a draining spoon and put into a glass or pale china dish, together with the walnuts. Flavour the prune cooking liquid with sherry, then add honey to taste – it should not be too sweet. Cool and pour over the prunes and walnuts. Serve chilled with whipped cream blended with thick yoghourt, and Spiced Almond Shortcakes.

Spiced Almond Shortcakes

100g (4oz) unsalted butter
50g (2oz) caster sugar
200g (7oz) plain flour
75g (3oz) ground almonds
1 egg
50g (2oz) icing sugar
1 teaspoon ground cinnamon
rose or orange flower water

In Greece these are called *kourabiedes*, in Spain *mantecados* or *polverones*. In fact they are dry crumbly biscuits made with ground almonds and flavoured with orange flower or rose water and cinnamon, a combination which reveals their Moorish origins.

Cream the butter with the sugar until light and fluffy, then add the egg with a sprinkling of flour and beat well. Knead in the flour and almonds until you have a firm dough. Pull off pieces about the size of a large walnut, shape into balls, flatten slightly on a greased baking sheet and make an indentation in each with a finger or thumb. Put in the fridge while the oven heats to 175°C/350°F/Gas 4. Bake the biscuits for 20 minutes, until they are firm but not browned (if they begin to brown too much, lower the heat by 10°C/20°F). While they are still warm, sift the icing sugar and cinnamon together. Sprinkle the biscuits with rose or orange flower water and then roll them in the icing sugar. They will keep for a week or two in an airtight tin.

George III's Banquet

In the late eighteenth century, when this would have been a typical meal to serve your guests, all the dishes, with the exception of the trifle and the savoury, would have been put on the table at once, and not served as separate courses as we do now. I have made this combination with some thought as to how the dishes would go together, should you wish to offer service *à la française* rather than in sequence, or *à la russe*.

Mrs Glasse's Stewed Scallops

8 large scallops and their coral
25g (1oz) butter
4 tablespoons medium
    dry white wine
pinch mace
juice of 2 Seville oranges
1 tablespoon flour worked to
    a paste with 25g (1oz) soft
    butter
3–4 tablespoons double cream
salt

This is an expensive dish, but then this is a celebration. In January, when I composed this menu, I bought both Seville oranges and asparagus, along with scallops. Failing Seville oranges, use a mixture of fresh lemon and orange juice. Failing scallops, use diced monk fish.

Remove the 'garter' which unites the white flesh of the scallop with its coral, and then slice the white part. Melt the butter, add the pieces of scallop and coral and cook briskly over a medium heat until they become opaque. Add the wine and the mace and cook at a brisk simmer for 3 minutes, then add the strained Seville orange juice. Remove the pieces of scallop with a draining spoon and put on a warmed dish. Add the flour and butter paste bit by bit to the simmering sauce, whisking until it is thick and glossy. Cook for at least a minute until it no longer tastes of raw flour, then add the cream and cook for a further minute. Season with a little salt

and pour over the scallops. Serve with a border of triangles of bread fried in a mixture of butter and oil, drained on kitchen paper and kept warm in a low oven with the door ajar to stop them going soggy.

Spinach with Orange

1·5kg (3lb) fresh spinach or
   450g (1lb) frozen leaf spinach
50g (2oz) butter
juice of 1 orange
1 orange cut into 8 wedges
salt, pepper and nutmeg

Remove the toughest ribs from the spinach and discard. Wash the rest thoroughly. Put it in a large heavy pan with no water except that which remains from the washing, and bring it to a boil over a high heat. Put a lid on the pan and boil hard for about 5 minutes, stirring from time to time as it cooks down, and adding a few meagre sprinkles of salt as it does so. When it has reduced to manageable proportions, tip it into a colander and cut it across and across with a sharp knife, put a plate on top and weigh it down to squeeze as much moisture as possible from it. If using frozen spinach, cook as directed and drain as above. Melt the butter in the pan in which the spinach cooked and add the orange juice. Return the spinach to the pan and cook fast, stirring all the time, until spinach, butter and orange juice are well mixed. Season with a little salt, if needed, freshly ground black pepper and a scrap of nutmeg. Serve surrounded with the orange wedges.

Duck Braised with Green Peas

2 Barbary ducks
2kg (4lb) fresh peas
   if available or
   1kg (2lb) frozen peas if not
600ml (1pt) good mild chicken
   stock
50g (2oz) butter
1 tablespoon sunflower oil
salt and freshly ground pepper
bunch of herbs – thyme, sage,
   parsley, celery, strip lemon
   peel

Barbary ducks are admirable for this recipe, as their flavour and lack of fat (compared with the Aylesbury variety) make them ideal for braising. Duck with green peas is a classic English combination which we have allowed to lapse – a fan of underdone duck breast with a few semi-raw mange-touts is not the same thing at all.

Heat the oven to 175°C/350°F/Gas 4. Season the ducks inside and out with salt and pepper. Brown them well all over in the butter and oil, then put in a casserole with the bunch of herbs. Shell the fresh peas, if using. Blanch either fresh or frozen peas for 1 minute in boiling salted water, drain well

and add to the ducks in the casserole. Pour the hot stock over all, cover with foil and then the lid and put in the oven. Cook for 45 minutes and check to see how they are doing – if you are using an earthenware casserole and/or the ducks are tightly packed, they will need another 15 minutes. If you are using cast iron and/or there is plenty of space around the birds, they will probably be tender and a leg or wing will part easily from the rest of the body. Dish them side by side on a large platter, remove the peas from the casserole with a slotted spoon and arrange them round the ducks. Reduce the juices by fast boiling and strain into a warmed gravy boat. Serve with new (or newish, depending on the season) potatoes, and asparagus.

Asparagus

2 bunches (700g/ 1½lb)
    asparagus
75g (3oz) butter
2 tablespoons fresh
    breadcrumbs

Snap off the bottom third or quarter of each stem and keep to flavour a soup. Steam the remainder until tender – not *al dente*, but soft without being soggy. Arrange on a flat dish and keep warm with a butter paper over the top. Fry the bread-crumbs in the butter until crisp. Scatter over the asparagus.

A Fine Trifle

14 trifle sponges, sliced
    horizontally
6 tablespoons sherry
200g (7oz) good quality apricot
    jam, sieved and warmed
600ml (1pt) creamy milk
1 strip lemon peel
1 vanilla pod
3 tablespoons sugar
3 large eggs
1 tablespoon cornflour
300ml (½pt) whipping cream
angelica
toasted flaked almonds
ratafias

Trifles had a bad press when they were made with packet custard, rubbery jelly, tinned fruit cocktail and hundreds-and-thousands; just as we had relearnt how to make them properly, they were given the thumbs down as being rich, creamy and therefore very wicked. This is one of the wicked variety, but as you will not be eating it every day it will do no lasting harm. George III would have been familiar with trifles like this.

Arrange the sliced sponge cakes on a large flattish dish and spoon the sherry over them. Leave to soak for an hour or so. If they are still a bit dry, add a little milk to soften them further. Pour the warmed jam over the top as evenly as possible. Make the custard by beating the eggs, sugar and cornflour together in a bowl. Bring the milk slowly to the boil, together with the lemon peel and vanilla pod, and when

it has almost boiled, pour it (with the lemon peel and vanilla pod) slowly on to the eggs, stirring all the time. Return this mixture to the pan and cook over a low heat until the custard is thick enough to coat the back of the spoon. Because this custard contains cornflour, it is unlikely to curdle and you can treat it quite casually. Strain it into a jug and leave it to cool a little, then pour over the sponge cakes. Leave until completely cold. Whip the cream, using a chilled bowl and beaters, until thick and spoon it gently over the custard. Decorate by sticking the almonds, angelica and ratafias carefully into the cream (they will sink if you lay them flat) just before serving.

A Cheese Savoury

100g (4oz) Cheshire or
   Cheddar cheese, grated
25g (1oz) butter
yolk of 1 hard-boiled egg
4 slices good quality white bread

This recipe, from Mrs Raffald's *The Experienced English House-keeper* published in 1794, is admirable in its simplicity. It can be prepared well ahead and popped under the grill just before serving.

'Take some old Cheshire-cheese, a lump of butter, and the yolk of a hard-boiled egg, and beat it very well together in a marble mortar, spread on some slices of bread toasted and buttered; hold a salamander over them and send them up.' I add some extra seasoning, in the form of a little salt and plenty of pepper, and do not butter the toast.

The Queen Mother's Lunch

Salmon Trout with a Green Sauce
Poulet au Riz
Raspberry Mousse with Peaches

for twelve

Variations on this lovely simple menu have been served at celebrations for the last 40 years. But rather than just follow the classic recipes for the three dishes, I have updated them a little. The green sauce for the salmon is a green peppercorn vinaigrette seasoned with lime juice. The rice for the chicken is a mixture of wild rice and basmati, each offering its own distinctive flavour. The raspberry mousse has a faint trace of orange and is made entirely without eggs, so is safe even in the warmest weather, and is served with slices of poached peach and a raspberry sauce.

Salmon Trout with a Green Sauce

1 salmon trout weighing about 1·5–2kg (3–4lb)
2 tablespoons light olive oil
salt and freshly ground black pepper
6 tablespoons white wine

FOR THE VINAIGRETTE SAUCE

180ml (7fl oz) light olive oil
juice of 1½ limes
2 dessertspoons green peppercorns in brine, drained and crushed
salt
finely chopped fresh coriander

Cook the salmon trout in foil in the oven, as on page 24, omitting the fennel and seasoning the fish inside and out with salt and pepper. Add the white wine, then fold the edges of the foil firmly together to seal.

When the cooked fish is nearly cold skin and bone it. Then arrange it in neat portions on individual plates. To make the vinaigrette, put all the ingredients except the coriander into a blender or processor and whizz to a thick emulsion – taste for salt and the balance of lime juice to oil, adding more of one or the other until it is to your taste (sharp, but not too sharp). Pour a neat circle of vinaigrette around each portion of fish, and garnish with finely chopped fresh coriander, plus a whole leaf or two. Serve with buttered brown bread.

Poulet au Riz

A simple dish of chicken in a creamy sauce served with rice. Prepare the rice ahead (see below), so you can concentrate on the sauce at the last minute. This dish is also good cold.

2 x 1·75kg (3½lb) free-range
   chickens, with giblets if
   possible
2 medium onions
2 carrots
2 sticks celery
bunch of herbs – parsley, thyme,
   bayleaf, strip lemon rind
2 cloves
2 cloves garlic
300ml (½pt) white wine or cider
water – about 1·75l (3pt)
salt
1 teaspoon black peppercorns

FOR THE RICE

225g (8oz) each wild rice
   and brown rice
about 900ml (1½pt) chicken
   stock – see method
finely chopped fresh tarragon

FOR THE SAUCE

900ml (1½pt) chicken stock
   – see method
85g (3oz) flour
90g (3½oz) butter
6 tablespoons crème fraîche
thread lemon juice
salt, freshly ground pepper,
   pinch nutmeg
2–3 teaspoons finely chopped
   fresh tarragon
some whole tarragon leaves

Season the chickens inside with salt and pepper, then put in a large pan with the flavouring vegetables and herbs, the peeled onions stuck with the cloves, the white wine and enough water to cover by about 1cm (½in). Add the giblets too, if you have them, but not the livers, which will make the stock cloudy and possibly bitter. A preserving pan with a lid of foil does perfectly well for this if you do not have a large enough saucepan. Bring up to the boil, then simmer gently for about 50–60 minutes, until the birds are tender. They are cooked when a leg pulls away easily. Remove them from the stock and carve into neat serving pieces, taking off the skin. Arrange on a large warmed dish and cover with foil. Keep warm while you finish off the rice and make the sauce.

Cook the rice earlier in the day. Wash the wild rice in a sieve under running water, then put it in a saucepan, pour over enough boiling water to cover it by 1cm (½in), simmer it for 5 minutes, then take off the heat, cover and leave for at least 1½ hours to cook in its own time. Do the same with the brown rice, but simmer it for 10 minutes and then let it stand for at least 2 hours. Drain both rices and combine. When the chicken is cooked, put the rice in a pan and add enough chicken stock to moisten, about 300ml (½pt), and a generous seasoning of salt and freshly ground black pepper. Put the pan over a low heat and simmer gently, uncovered, until the stock has been absorbed. This method ensures that both types of rice are properly cooked (their cooking times vary) and that they are well-flavoured with the stock. Fork in the tarragon and, if serving hot, a generous nut of butter. If cold, then simply make sure that the rice is not too dry by adding a little extra stock. If you have a large enough serving dish, put the rice around the chicken, otherwise serve it separately.

To make the sauce, take 900ml (1½pt) of the hot chicken stock. Melt the butter over a low heat, off the heat stir in the flour, then return to the heat and cook for another minute,

before adding the stock gradually, stirring all the time. Raise the heat a little and bring the sauce to a steady simmer. Cook for about 5 minutes, until the taste of raw flour has gone. Add the cream and the seasoning, then the lemon juice and finally the tarragon. Pour over the chicken and garnish with whole tarragon leaves.

This dish needs no potatoes, of course, but tiny carrots tossed in butter and seasoned with a squeeze of lemon juice and a dusting of parsley are ideal partners. If serving cold, a crisp green salad is all you need.

Raspberry Mousse with Peaches

FOR THE MOUSSE

1kg (2¼lb) fresh raspberries
600ml (1pt) whipping cream
180ml (8fl oz) fresh orange juice
2 sachets gelatine
40g (1½oz) caster sugar
mint leaves

FOR THE SAUCE

500g (1lb) fresh or frozen raspberries
100g (4oz) caster sugar
1 teaspoon orange flower water

FOR THE PEACHES

6 ripe peaches
600ml (1pt) water
225g (8oz) sugar
1 tablespoon (approx.) orange flower water
squeeze lemon juice

First make the mousse. Sprinkle the gelatine on to the orange juice in a small saucepan. Leave it for a minute or two to form a sponge, then put it over a low heat to dissolve – do not let it boil. Set aside 24 perfect raspberries for the garnish, then liquidise or process the rest, sieve them and stir in the sugar and the melted gelatine, taste to check if you need more sugar, then process again. Whip the cream in a chilled bowl with chilled beaters until thick and billowy, then fold into the raspberry mixture. Pour into a bowl, cover with cling film and leave to set.

Make the sauce by processing the raspberries and sugar and sieving to get rid of the pips. Stir in the orange flower water. Refrigerate.

Make the syrup for the peaches by bringing the water and sugar slowly to the boil and simmering fast for 15 minutes. Leave to cool, then stir in the orange flower water and lemon juice. Skin the peaches by dipping each one briefly into a pan of boiling water – the skins will slip off easily. Slice each peach into 8 segments and drop them into the syrup. Cover and refrigerate.

To assemble this dessert, take spoonfuls of the mousse and arrange two on a pool of the sauce with a fan of peach slices. Decorate with mint leaves and whole raspberries. Use a well-shaped spoon to form the mousse. It helps if you dip the spoon in warm water each time, shaking off the water before scooping up the mousse.

ROMANTIC
TRIUMPHS

ROMANTIC TRIUMPHS

Arranged marriages, to secure the union of estates as part of a betrothal settlement, were an important part of social life among the upper echelons of society for many hundreds of years. Though the wedding feasts might be triumphant, there was little romance about these carefully planned weddings, which could be as calculating as any boardroom takeover.

The union of wealth and politics celebrated at the wedding of Henrietta Cavendish-Holles and Edward, Lord Harley, which took place at *Wimpole Hall*, Cambridgeshire, in 1713 was typical, but it was unusual in that it was also a love match. In contrast, at *Hanbury Hall* in Worcestershire the heiress of the estate had married Henry Cecil, heir to the 9th Earl of Exeter, in 1776. Together they wasted their inheritance and he neglected his wife who promptly fell in love and then eloped with the local curate. The chagrined Cecil deserted Hanbury and his creditors and emerged, under a new name, in a quiet Shropshire village. Lodging with a farmer, he seduced the farmer's daughter and a shotgun wedding followed. Cecil resolved his bigamy by a secret divorce from his first wife and marrying his second, again, at a London ceremony. When, two years later, he inherited the title, he told his wife nothing but took her to the Cecil family seat at Burghley in Lincolnshire, where she found to her surprise that she was greeted with the deepest respect by the servants. She never quite got over the shock of such a steep social climb, and the story of the 'cottage countess' is told with great inaccuracy but much romantic verve by Tennyson in *The Lord of Burghley*.

If that is a fine example of a 'rags to riches' love story, so too is that of Sir Harry Fetherstonhaugh's marrage in 1825, late in his life, to his dairy maid, Mary Ann. She cared for him devotedly until his death in 1846, aged ninety-two, and then cared for his house, *Uppark*, in Sussex, with equal devotion until her own death many years later.

An elopement at *Lacock Abbey* was noted by John Aubrey in his *Brief Lives*. Olive, youngest daughter of Henry Sharington, jumped from the 'Battlements of the Abbey-Church' and, landing rather heavily on her lover, John Talbot, despite the fact that the wind caught her petticoats 'and did somewhat breake the fall', knocked him unconscious. 'Her father told her that since she had made such a leap she

should e'en marrie him'; she outlived both her husband and her son, dying at Lacock in 1646 'being about an hundred years old'.

A romantic liaison which was brought to an end in 1735 is commemorated at *Felbrigg*, in Norfolk, where a verse inscribed with a diamond on a window pane testifies to the passionate love felt by Benjamin Stillingfleet, tutor to William Windham, for the sister of the Rector of Felbrigg. And the delightful *Mussenden Temple*, County Londonderry, was built as the result of an infatuation for his young and beautiful cousin, Frideswide Mussenden, by the very eccentric Frederick Hervey, 4th Earl of Bristol, Bishop of Derry and builder of *Ickworth* in Suffolk. Tragically, Frideswide died aged 22 in 1785 (the year of the Temple's completion), shortly after the storm of scandal about her association with Frederick Hervey broke.

Considerably less dashing, but equally poignant, was Philip Yorke's courting of Louisa Scott, at *Erddig*, in 1902. He had been unhappily married for many years to a woman who deserted him soon after their wedding. She died when he was 50, leaving him free to marry again, but despite inviting a bevy of eligible ladies to a succession of house parties at Erddig, and proposing to each as they left by way of a prettily packaged verse, none took up the challenge. None, that is, until the sportive Miss Scott, a fellow cycling enthusiast and daughter of the Rev. T. J. Scott of Chilton Foliat in Wiltshire, succumbed to his mature charms. She wrote in her diary on St Valentine's Day: 'One of the happiest days of my life. Mr Yorke and I walked to Wrexham and coming home he said such pretty things to me and called me his "sister". . . . In the evening we learned Palmistry and at 12.15, under the picture of the former Philip Yorke [by Gainsborough] he asked me.'

An Elopement Supper or Valentine's Day Repast

Mushrooms in a Truffled Dressing
Breast of Chicken en Papillote with Love Apples
Coeurs à la Crème with Passion Fruit Sauce

for two

This is not a meal you can take with you while eloping, but you might consider it once you are safely away. It is ideal as a Valentine's Day (or Wedding Anniversary) lunch or dinner as only the middle course need divert your attention.

Mushrooms in a Truffled Dressing

100g (4oz) button mushrooms
100g (4oz) oyster mushrooms
1 tablespoon light olive oil
2 tablespoons sherry
bayleaf
2 dessertspoons truffle oil
salt, freshly ground pepper
3 drops Tabasco, or a pinch
* of cayenne*
2 slices good quality white bread
few leaves pink radicchio

This calls for truffle oil, which is very expensive but fragrant with the (supposedly) aphrodisiac aroma of the truffle. It is available from delicatessens and good food shops.

Tiny button mushrooms are best because they can be left whole. If they are larger, halve or quarter them. Wipe clean, but do not wash or peel them. Cut the oyster mushrooms into neat pieces. Sauté both in the olive oil over a medium heat, until they begin to exude juice. Add the sherry, bayleaf, a sprinkling of salt and a grinding of pepper, then lower the heat. Cook for a further 10 minutes until tender. Spoon into a dish and, while still warm, dress with a dessertspoonful of the truffle oil and the Tabasco or cayenne. Leave to cool. Cut the bread into two heart shapes, do it free-hand if you are good at that sort of thing, or use a heart-shaped cutter. Sprinkle with the remaining dessertspoon of truffle oil, then grill until crisp. Leave on a rack. Just before serving put one on each plate and spoon the mushrooms on top. Garnish with the pink radicchio leaves.

Breast of Chicken en Papillote with Love Apples

2 boned and skinned chicken
    breasts
50g (2oz) butter
4 large 'grown-for-flavour'
    tomatoes
2 teaspoons balsamic vinegar
sunflower oil
salt and freshly ground pepper
2 sheets of foil, about 26cm
    (10in) square

Love apples, of course, are tomatoes, which, when they first appeared in this country, were believed to have aphrodisiac properties. Cooking the chicken in an envelope of foil makes this potentially dry meat moist and succulent – and reduces the unromantic washing-up afterwards.

Fold the sheets of foil in half and mark out half a heart-shape along the fold. Cut round the outline and open out the foil to the full heart shape. This is not just romantic fantasy – it is an ideal shape for enclosing the tapering chicken breast. Heat the oven to 200°C/400°F/Gas 6. Skin the tomatoes by dipping them briefly into boiling water, slitting the skin and slipping it off. Cut in quarters, remove all seeds and dice. Season the chicken breasts, then fry them quickly on both sides in the oil, just long enough to seal the meat and give it a pale golden colour. Place each one on one half of a foil heart and add half the tomato, half the butter and half the balsamic vinegar, plus a little salt and pepper. Fold the other side of the heart over and pinch the sides together firmly. Place on a baking sheet and bake for 25 minutes. The hearts should be opened at table, on to hot plates. There will be plenty of buttery, tomatoey juice, so serve some Pink Fir Apple potatoes (available from good greengrocers and super-markets) boiled in their skins, then finished in a little butter with torn fresh basil to give extra aroma. A green salad goes well with this.

Coeurs à la Crème with Passion Fruit Sauce

175g (6oz) fromage frais
150ml (¼pt) double cream
1 tablespoon vanilla sugar

FOR THE SAUCE
6 ripe passion fruit
sugar to taste

You will need four of the small or one of the large pierced china heart-shaped dishes made expressly for this purpose, which can be bought from cookware shops. The coeurs should be made several hours in advance to allow them to drain thoroughly.

Line the mould(s) with damp muslin, clean handkerchiefs, or new J-cloths, pressing the cloth well down over the inside

so the shape is not lost when you turn them out. Whip the cream a little to add to its bulk, then fold in the fromage frais and sugar until thoroughly blended. Spoon into the lined mould(s) and place on a plate. Leave in a cool place to drain for at least 4 hours. Make the sauce by pushing the pulp from the passion fruit through a sieve to get rid of the pips. Season to taste with a little sugar, much will depend on how ripe the fruit is; the more wrinkled the skins, the riper and sweeter they will be. Stir until the sugar dissolves. To serve, turn out the hearts on to two plates, remove the muslin and pour a little of the sauce around them. If making one large heart, turn out on to a single plate and surround with the sauce.

Feast for an Arranged Marriage

Consommé Viveur
Rôti Sans-pareil
Broad Bean and Anchovy Salad
Artichoke, Celery and Tomato Salad
Orange Blossom Tipsy Cake

for twenty-four

Today's wedding 'breakfast' is more often a lunch, which is the intention behind this menu. The 'Queen Mother's Lunch' on page 106 would be equally suitable. The first two recipes are based on two from a book which was reviewed as both 'the most pathetic of all cookery books in its futility' and as 'a monument of ripe scholarship and sardonic enthusiasm' when it came out in 1952. Called *Venus in the Kitchen*, and edited by Norman Douglas, with an introduction by Graham Greene, it was a collection of recipes with supposedly aphrodisiac qualities. Why a consommé flavoured with celery or a multi-bird roast should be regarded as aphrodisiac I cannot think, but Consommé Viveur is described as 'very stimulating indeed'. Whether it is or not, it makes a good beginning to a wedding lunch.

Consommé Viveur

turkey, chicken and duck
   carcases – see method
500g (1lb) shin beef
2 large onions
4 large carrots, split
4 sticks celery
generous bunch herbs – parsley,
   sage, thyme, bayleaf, lemon
   peel
3·5 l (6pt) water
2 teaspoons peppercorns
4 cloves
salt

TO FINISH

2 celery hearts, finely sliced,
   leaves and all
300ml ($\frac{1}{2}$pt) crème fraîche
finely chopped fresh chervil
   or parsley

This uses the bones from the poultry in the next recipe. Make the stock a day ahead so you can skim the fat from the top.

Break up the bones a little so that they fit in a large pan, then add the beef, cut into rough chunks, and all the other flavourings. Leave the skin on the onions to make the stock a rich golden brown. Add the water. Bring slowly to the boil, skim off any froth which comes to the surface, then lower the heat and simmer gently for about 2 hours. Strain the stock into a large bowl or jug and leave to cool. Next day, skim off the fat and reheat the stock. Taste to check if it needs further salt. Strain again through a sieve lined with muslin or a new J-cloth, then put into the pan with the finely sliced celery. Bring up to a simmer and simmer for about 10 minutes. Strain out the celery and reserve for the stuffing in the Rôti Sans-pareil below. If serving cold, put the consommé into bowls or soup cups and add a teaspoon of cream and a scattering of chervil or parsley to each. If serving hot, reheat without boiling, put into bowls and add the cream and herbs.

Note
The beef from the consommé-making is excellent dealt with in the French manner. Mix it with a mustardy vinaigrette, some finely chopped shallots and parsley, and serve it either with baked potatoes or as a sandwich filling.

Rôti Sans-pareil

1 turkey, 5·5–6kg (12lb)
1 large duck, about 3kg (6lb)
1 free-range chicken, about 2kg
   (4lb)

FOR THE STUFFING

500g (1lb) boned shoulder pork
celery from the consommé
1 large mild Spanish onion,
   finely diced
50g (2oz) fresh brown
   breadcrumbs
1 large egg
3 tablespoons pistachio nuts,
   roughly chopped
grated rind 1 lemon
½ teaspoon ground allspice
salt and freshly ground black
   pepper
3 tablespoons finely chopped
   parsley
dripping or good olive oil

Norman Douglas's 'aphrodisiac' dish started with an olive as the stuffing for a garden warbler and ended, bird within bird, with a turkey enclosed in a bustard. This scaled-down version makes use of the most easily available domestic poultry – the chicken, duck and turkey. All three must be boned, but this is really quite easy. It can be done whenever convenient and the boned birds stored in the freezer until 24 hours before you begin cooking. It also has the advantage of providing the carcases to make the consommé – which can be made ahead and frozen too.

Bone all the birds in the same way: cut off the last joint of the wings and save for the consommé. Place the bird breast down on a firm surface and, with a sharp knife, cut down along the spine, through the skin and flesh to the bone. With the tip of the knife, but keeping the blade flat against the carcase, ease the flesh away from the bones. When you meet the ball and socket joints where the thighs and wings join the body, ease these away and continue to follow round until you reach the breast. When you bone the turkey be careful at this point because the bone is so near the skin it is easy to make a hole. This does not matter with the duck and chicken, as they will be encased within the turkey. Continue round until you can lift the carcase away from the skin and flesh. Return to the legs and wings, and ease the wing and thigh bones away and out. On the turkey, leave the drumsticks intact as they help to give the roast a convincing shape, but remove them from the duck and chicken.

To make the stuffing, cook the onion in a little well-flavoured dripping if you have it, or some good olive oil if not, until soft and golden. Mince the pork. Mix together all the remaining ingredients, using the egg to bind everything. Assemble the roast: place the chicken skin side down and season with salt and black pepper. Arrange the pork and celery stuffing down the centre and fold the chicken around it to make a neat bolster shape. Turn spare flaps of skin to the inside. Place the duck skin side down and season as before. Again, turn any wing, leg or neck flaps of skin to the inside.

117

Put the chicken bolster in the middle and wrap the duck around it, encasing it neatly. Place the turkey skin side down and season. Place the duck/chicken bolster in the centre and, again, turn any spare skin to the inside. Enfold the bolster in the turkey and this time stitch the skin together down the back, using either a needle and thread or metal skewers. Do not pull too tight or it will burst with the strain of the expanding breadcrumbs in the stuffing.

Weigh the roast and calculate its cooking time. Rub with olive oil and salt and place on a rack in the roasting tin. As this is now solid meat, without bones to conduct heat, it will take a long time to cook. Allow 25 minutes per pound, plus 15 minutes, at a temperature of 200°C/400°F/Gas 6 for the first hour, lowering the heat to 160°C/325°F/Gas 3 for the rest of the cooking time. As the fat begins to flow, after about 45 minutes, begin to baste assiduously – the fat in the duck will lubricate the chicken, and the interior of the turkey, but the turkey's white breast meat needs help from you.

When cooked, remove the skewers or thread as soon as it is cool enough to handle, then leave to cool in the coldest place you can find.

To serve, simply carve across in neat slices and partner with the following salads.

Broad Bean and Anchovy Salad

Cook 1·5kg (3lb) frozen broad beans until tender, cool a little then slip off the tough greyish skins. Dress with a generous quantity of vinaigrette to which you have added 2 tins finely chopped anchovy fillets – and their oil. Sprinkle with parsley.

Artichoke, Celery and Tomato Salad

Use 2kg (4½lb) tomatoes and 2 tins of celery hearts, rinsed of their brine and drained on paper towels, plus a jar of artichoke hearts in oil. Toss in a vinaigrette made with olive oil and lemon juice and add torn basil leaves.

Orange Blossom Tipsy Cake

550g (1¼lb) self-raising flour
550g (1¼lb) golden caster sugar
8 eggs, separated
350ml (12fl oz) sunflower oil
grated rind of 2 oranges
170ml (6fl oz) orange juice
170ml (6fl oz) milk

FOR THE TIPSY SYRUP

450ml (¾pt) orange juice
honey to sweeten
6 tablespoons Cointreau

FOR THE CUSTARD

600ml (1pt) full-cream milk
600ml (1pt) single cream
5 egg yolks
100g (4oz) caster sugar
orange flower water to taste
300ml (½pt) slightly sweetened
    whipped cream

Tipsy cake was popular at celebrations both rustic and pa-
trician during the last century. Basically a sponge cake soaked
in alcohol, and usually sitting in a lake of custard, it differed
from a trifle by being both more alcoholic and rather less
rich in cream. This recipe is an orange sponge cake soaked in
a mixture of Cointreau and orange juice – to make it less
alcoholic for drivers – surrounded by a rich custard flavoured
with orange flower water. The variations, however, are
endless. A coffee sponge soaked in coffee and brandy and
partnered with a chocolate custard, is also excellent. The
cake is easy to make and is best made ahead of time and
allowed to mellow for 24 hours, thus relieving pressure on
the cook. It looks very good baked in a ring mould, which
also gives nice-sized slices and makes it seem more like a
dessert and less like a cake. This recipe fills three 23cm (9in)
ring moulds.

Grease and flour the ring moulds, and heat the oven to
175°C/350°F/Gas 4. Whisk together the egg yolks, sunflower oil, milk and orange juice. In a large bowl mix the
flour and sugar together and make a well in the centre. Pour
in the egg/oil mixture and beat well, adding the grated
orange rind. Whip the egg whites until stiff and fold in carefully until well blended. Pour into the prepared ring moulds
and bake for 35–40 minutes, or until well-risen and firm
and beginning to come away from the sides of the moulds.
Turn on to a cake rack to cool a little while you make the
syrup.

Warm the orange juice and add enough honey to sweeten
very slightly – just to take the acid edge off the flavour –
make sure the honey has melted completely, then add the
Cointreau. Put the cakes into plastic cake boxes or tins, and
pour the syrup slowly over them until they are well soaked.
Leave overnight.

Make the custard. Combine the egg yolks and sugar in a
bowl. Bring the milk and cream just up to the boil, then pour
onto the egg yolks in a steady stream, stirring all the time.
Return the mixture to the rinsed-out pan over a very low

heat and cook slowly, stirring all the time, until the custard is thick enough to coat the back of a spoon. Remove from the heat and stir in enough orange flower water to add a subtle flavour – too much and it will taste like face-cream. Pour into a jug and press cling film onto the surface to prevent a skin forming.

About an hour before serving, place the cakes on shallow serving dishes and surround each with a moat of the custard. Pipe the whipped cream in a coronet around the top of each cake and stick blanched, toasted almonds upright all round, *à la* Mrs Beeton, or decorate with imitation orange blossom and silver leaves, or both.

FINE TEAS

FINE TEAS

At *Arlington Court*, on the North Devon coast, the table is laid in the dining room for afternoon tea, rather than the more usual formal dinner. The delicate mauve of the china is echoed in the hand-embroidered napkins, each decorated with an anchor – to reflect Miss Rosalie Chichester's family connections with the sea and all things nautical. You can hardly fail to miss the seafaring element elsewhere in the house. Sea paintings, model ships, shells brought back from foreign shores fill every available space. In fact, Miss Chichester's tea parties were famous for miles around, and it is more than likely that Canon Rawnsley, one of the three founders of the National Trust in 1895 and a friend of Miss Chichester, was a frequent guest. When she inherited the Arlington estate from her mother in 1908 Miss Chichester gave the first of several gifts of land on the coast to the Trust in memory of her parents.

In the wonderfully appointed kitchens at *Lanhydrock House*, in Cornwall, there is a special scalding range in the Dairy Scullery for the making of scalded (or clotted) cream. The 6th Viscount Clifden rebuilt the house after the disastrous fire in 1881 to provide a simple family home for his nine children; clotted cream must have been a feature of at least some of their birthday teas.

Clotted cream was certainly a feature of the cricket teas held at *Knightshayes Court* in Devon. In her book *Good Things in England*, published in 1932, Florence White remembers 'when Blundell's School played some other Eleven, and whether they won or lost Blundell's boys piled thick rich cream on to thick slices of plum cake, or trickled golden syrup over substantial slices of bread and cream which they called "thunder and lightning" or stuck a spoonful of luscious strawberry jam in the centre of a split Chudleigh already thickly spread with scalded . . . cream.'

In *The Servants' Hall*, his excellent book on *Erddig*, Clwyd, Merlin Waterson introduces the Yorke family with the endearing information that, 'While the last Philip Yorke was squire of Erddig, the most important room in the house was the Servants' Hall, the most important meal, tea.' Everyone, whoever they were, whatever their status, was entertained in that comfortably cluttered and daily shabbier room, to 'mounds of bread and butter, jam and cakes'. Less enticingly, tea in the housekeeper's room at *Uppark*, Sussex, where Mrs Wells reigned in the 1880s, has been

immortalised in her son's H. G. Wells' autobiographical novel *Tono-Bungay*, in which Uppark on the South Downs is thinly disguised as Bladesover on the Kentish Downs: 'I hated teatime in the housekeeper's room more than anything else at Bladesover.' The young hero particularly hated it when three pensioned-off servants returned on their annual visit and 'sat about . . . eating great quantities of cake, drinking much tea in a stately manner and reverberating remarks.'

In a recent article for the National Trust *Magazine* Anthea Mander Lahr, daughter of Rosalie Mander and Sir Geoffrey Mander who gave *Wightwick Manor*, near Wolverhampton, to the National Trust, throws a harshly realistic light on the nursery life there. Now the nursery is set out as a haven of childhood memories, but then it was very different: 'Frugal meals consisted of eggs, baked beans, cheese dreams, roes and creamed haddock (my favourite) . . . this diet I supplemented by making condensed-milk sandwiches . . . .' One cold spring afternoon we were being given one of Lady Mander's inimitable tours of her beloved house. 'And now for some tea' she said hospitably, when we had explored every pre-Raphaelite nook and cranny and, indeed, from somewhere deep in the house came the smell of toasting – crumpets, perhaps, or cinnamon toast. But we were ushered into the dining room and honoured with chilly sandwiches and damp cake while our breath and the tea-cups steamed in the inadequately heated air. Meanwhile, in the kitchen, the lucky staff feasted on those crumpets, that toast.

A good combination for a christening tea, would be shrimp sandwiches, asparagus sandwiches (page 130), macaroons (page 132), and the rum and raisin cake from this menu, made with dark brown sugar and marzipanned and iced traditionally.

A Yachting Tea for Miss Chichester, Canon Rawnsley and Selected Guests

Anchovy Toast
Shrimp and Seaweed Sandwiches
Sand Cake
Boiled Rum and Raisin Cake

Anchovy Toast

1 tin anchovy fillets, drained
100g (4oz) unsalted butter,
  soft but not melted
4 drops Tabasco sauce

If you like, cover the anchovy fillets in milk and soak for an hour to draw out some of the fishy flavour. I prefer to use them as they are, blotting off their oil with kitchen paper. Chop the fillets roughly and blend until smooth with the butter and Tabasco. Pack into a small pot and refrigerate until required. Spread thinly on slices of hot toast and stack on a plate set over a bowl of hot water to keep warm.

Shrimp and Seaweed Sandwiches

200g (7oz) carton potted
  shrimps
$\frac{1}{2}$ lemon
bunch of watercress
1 fine sliced wholemeal
  loaf, thinly buttered

Cut off the stems of the watercress just above the rubber band and wash the leaves. Dry well in a salad spinner or tea cloth. Turn the potted shrimps into a bowl and add a generous squeeze of lemon juice, then mix all together with a fork, being careful not to break up the shrimps too much. Spread a slice of bread with some of the shrimp mixture, cover with some watercress (seaweed) and top with another slice of bread. Press it lightly but firmly with the palm of your hand, then trim off the crusts.

Sand Cake

175g (6oz) each plain flour,
  golden caster sugar and soft
  butter
50g (2oz) ground almonds
2 large eggs
$\frac{1}{2}$ teaspoon baking powder
grated rind $\frac{1}{2}$ lemon

FOR THE TOPPING

50g (2oz) blanched almonds,
  coarsely chopped
25g (1oz) demerara sugar
2 teaspoons cinnamon

This has the texture of a madeira cake, but with a sandy, crumbly topping of chopped almonds, cinnamon and sugar. It improves if kept for a day or two.

Grease and line a cake tin with a removable base. Heat the oven to 160°C/325°F/Gas 3. Cream the butter, sugar and lemon rind until light and fluffy. Beat in the eggs one at a time, each with a sprinkling of flour. Sift the rest of the flour with the baking powder, then mix with the ground almonds and fold into the creamed butter and eggs. Spoon into the cake tin and bake in the centre of the oven for 45 minutes. Mix together the ingredients for the topping. Open the door of the oven gently and pull the cake to the front. Spoon the topping over the top of the cake and slide the tin back into the oven to cook for a further 30 minutes. Cool the cake for about 15 minutes before removing it from the tin.

Boiled Rum and Raisin Cake

300ml (½pt) strained cold tea
6 tablespoons rum
275g (10oz) raisins
85g (3oz) sultanas
85g (3oz) dried cherries, or apricots, diced
225g (8oz) soft brown sugar
225g (8oz) soft margarine
350g (12oz) self-raising flour
3 eggs
2 teaspoons ground mace
2 teaspoons ground allspice

This is a very nautical cake, a richer variation of the Century Cake on page 47. It has a lovely light moist texture and plump fruit, thanks to the initial soaking of the raisins. 'Boiled' is the traditional name and just refers to the quick simmer you give the fruit before leaving it to soak.

Put the dried fruit into a large saucepan with the tea and simmer for about 5 minutes. Take the pan off the heat, stir in the rum, cover, and leave the fruit to soak overnight. Grease and line a 23cm (9in) cake tin. Heat the oven to 160°C/325°F/Gas 3. Beat the margarine and sugar together until creamy, then add the eggs, one at a time accompanied by a spoonful of flour, beating well, then stir in the fruit. Finally fold in the flour sifted with the spices. Spoon into the tin, hollow the top slightly then bake for 1½–2 hours, until the cake has shrunk a little and a metal skewer pushed into the centre comes out clean. Cool on a rack, then wrap in foil and keep for about a week before eating. If you want to add more rum, pierce the cake several times with a skewer while it is still warm and slowly pour another few tablespoons of rum over it – if you put the cake in its storage tin before you do this, any rum which runs off the top will eventually be absorbed. Or you can ice the cake with a rum-flavoured water icing instead.

A Cosy Kitchen Tea

Soda Bread and Butter
Blackberry Jelly
Vanilla Apple Butter
Welsh Cakes
Parkin

Soda Bread

200g (8oz) wholemeal flour
2 teaspoons baking powder
½ level teaspoon salt
1 level teaspoon demerara sugar
25g (1oz) margarine
150ml (¼pt) milk
  (or buttermilk)
cracked wheat

Soda bread is the best of all breads when eaten warm from the oven. It should be thickly spread with salty butter (Cornish or Welsh are my own preferences), overlaid with home-made jam. This recipe, by Mrs Edith Smith, comes from her collection of recipes using the stoneground flour produced at Park Mill, a stroll across the fields from *Bateman's*, Rudyard Kipling's beloved house near Burwash in Sussex.

Heat the oven to 200°C/400°F/Gas 6. Mix flour, salt, sugar and baking powder in a bowl. Rub in the margarine. Add the milk to make a soft dough. Shape into a round. Place on a greased baking sheet. Brush the top with milk, sprinkle with cracked wheat. Bake for 20–30 minutes.

Blackberry Jelly

2kg (4lb) blackberries
500ml (16fl oz) red wine
sugar, granulated or preserving

A recipe given to me by a French friend – the flavour of the wine is not obvious, but it does enhance the blackberries.

Put the blackberries and the wine in a preserving pan and cook gently until the fruit is completely soft. Tip into a jelly bag or old, clean pillowcase and suspend from a hook over a deep bowl. Leave to drip overnight. Next day, measure out the juice and add 350g (12oz) sugar for each pint of juice. Heat slowly, stirring until you can no longer feel the gritty sugar beneath the spoon, then raise the heat and boil fast until setting point is reached. To test for setting, put a scant teaspoonful of jelly on a saucer. Leave for a minute or two. Then push your finger across the surface – if it wrinkles, the jelly is ready. Pot in clean, warm, dry jars.

Vanilla Apple Butter

about 2kg (4½lb) apples, mixed cookers and eaters
300ml (½pt) dry cider or unsweetened apple juice
2 vanilla pods, cut into short lengths
sugar, granulated or preserving

This is thicker than jam and very finely flavoured. You can vary the flavourings – diced preserved ginger stirred in just before potting is very good or scented geranium leaves for a completely different effect. This is an excellent way of using up windfalls.

Wash the apples, remove any bruised or bad bits, then cut them up roughly and put them in a heavy pan with the cider or apple juice. Cover and cook gently until the apples are pulpy, then push through a sieve or a food mill. Weigh the purée into a large pan and add 350g (12oz) sugar for each 450g (1lb) fruit. Count the pieces of vanilla pod before adding them to the pan and stir well. Heat gently until the sugar dissolves. Raise the heat and cook, stirring all the time, until the surface bubbles. Simmer steadily for about 20–30 minutes, until the mixture is fairly stiff and a wooden spoon drawn through it leaves a path across the base of the pan. How long this takes depends on the type of apples and whether the growing season was a wet or dry one, because this, of course, affects the apples' moisture content. Remove all the pieces of vanilla pod, then pot the butter in clean, warm, dry jars. Rinse and dry the vanilla pieces and save them in an air-tight jar for reuse.

Welsh Cakes

225g (8oz) plain flour
100g (4oz) butter
85g (3oz) caster sugar
85g (3oz) currants
¼ teaspoon grated nutmeg
½ teaspoon cinnamon
½ teaspoon baking powder
1 egg, beaten
milk to mix if necessary

Makes eight large cakes.
These, I'm sure, must have appeared on that kitchen tea-table at *Erddig*, in Clwyd. They are delicious, whether fresh from the griddle, toasted, or simply cold, and with butter or without. I use a heavy cast-iron frying pan instead of a griddle.

Sift the flour with the baking powder and spices, then rub in the butter and stir in the currants and sugar. Mix to a soft dough with the egg, and the milk if necessary. Roll out on a floured board to about 5mm (¼in) thick and cut into circles with a large biscuit cutter. Heat the griddle or heavy frying pan, then grease it by wrapping a lump of lard in a piece of

muslin and wiping it quickly over the surface. Cook the Welsh cakes for about $2\frac{1}{2}$–3 minutes before turning and cooking the other side.

Parkin

450g (1lb) plain flour
225g (8oz) medium oatmeal
175g (6oz) soft brown sugar
$1\frac{1}{2}$ teaspoons ground ginger
2 teaspoons mixed spice
pinch salt
50g (2oz) mixed peel
50g (2oz) sultanas
scant 450ml ($\frac{3}{4}$pt) water
100g (4oz) lard
450g (1lb) mixed black treacle
   and golden syrup
$\frac{1}{2}$ teaspoon bicarbonate of soda
50g (2oz) blanched split
   almonds (optional)
1 tablespoon caster sugar
2 tablespoons hot water

When *Quarry Bank Mill*, at Styal in Cheshire, first opened as a museum in the 1970s, numbers of us volunteered to bake the cakes sold in the tea-room. This was my recipe for parkin, which I baked in quadruplicate every week. It is at its best a week after baking.

Heat the oven to 160°C/325°F/Gas 3. Remove the lids from the tins of treacle and syrup and stand them in the oven as it heats, so making the contents easier to pour. Line a shallow roasting tin with baking parchment. Mix together the first eight ingredients in a large bowl. Place a heavy-based saucepan on the scales and pour in the syrup and treacle – the proportions do not matter very much – to the required weight. Add the water and lard and put the pan over a low heat until the lard has melted, stirring until water, lard and syrups are well blended. Add the bicarbonate of soda and stir again, so that it froths up and pour the contents of the pan onto the dry ingredients. Mix very well; this mixture tends to conceal bubbles of unblended flour within itself, so be thorough. Pour into the prepared tin. If you are using the almonds – and they do add a nicely luxurious touch – arrange them in a pattern on the top, then bake for $1\frac{3}{4}$–2 hours until firm and springy. Dissolve the sugar in the hot water and brush the top while the parkin is still warm, then allow to cool in the tin. When cold, remove from the tin, wrap in greaseproof paper and foil and store for at least 2 days, but a week is better. Cut into squares or fingers.

A Polite Tea

Asparagus Sandwiches
Pondicherry Sandwiches
Rich Chocolate Cake
Royal Biscuits
Macaroons

This is the kind of tea which you offer in refined company; the sandwiches are tiny, their crusts removed, the cake is the centrepiece, surrounded by satellite plates of biscuits. Macaroons are a must. The tea should be carefully chosen to react with the local water – no shoving any old teabags into the pot. Choose Ceylon tea if you are in a soft-water area, Assam for harder water.

Asparagus Sandwiches

1 tin asparagus tips or
*   225g (8oz) cooked asparagus*
*   tips*
vinaigrette
1 thin-sliced brown loaf
soft butter

If using tinned asparagus drain it well. Marinate the tips in the vinaigrette for about 30 minutes. Butter the bread, trim off the crusts and cut each slice to the same length as the asparagus tips. Roll up 2–3 asparagus tips in each half-slice.

Pondicherry Sandwiches

3 eggs
mild chutney
curry powder
soft butter
salt
a good quality white loaf
mustard and cress

Cover the eggs with cold water, bring to the boil and boil for 10 minutes, 12 minutes if they were straight from the fridge. Immediately the cooking time is up, run cold water into the pan, then peel the eggs as soon as you can handle them. Doing this avoids the grey ring round the yolk, which would give a greyish tinge to the sandwiches. Mash them as finely as possible, with curry powder and salt to taste. Slice and butter the bread. Spread half the slices with chutney and the rest with the egg mixture. Press lightly together, then trim off the crusts. Garnish with mustard and cress.

Rich Chocolate Cake

120g (4½oz) top quality
    plain chocolate
175g (6oz) unsalted butter
175g (6oz) vanilla sugar
½ teaspoon cinnamon
few drops almond extract
grated rind of 1½ oranges
3 eggs
85g (3oz) plain flour
¾ teaspoon baking powder
175g (6oz) ground almonds

TO FINISH

85g (3oz) of the same chocolate
4 tablespoons marmalade, with
    peel sieved out

This is a dense, richly chocolatey cake, not a light-as-air confection full of baking powder, so do not expect it to rise much. What it lacks in height, however, it more than makes up for in depth of flavour.

Grease and flour a 24cm (10in) cake tin. Heat the oven to 170°C/350°F/Gas 4. Break up the chocolate and melt it in a bowl over a pan of gently simmering water. Beat the butter, sugar, cinnamon, almond extract and orange rind together until light, then beat in the eggs, one at a time, then the melted and slightly cooled chocolate. Beat hard for about half a minute. Mix together the flour, almonds and baking powder and fold this lightly into the chocolate mixture – do not beat any more. Pour into the cake tin and bake for about 1 hour (40 minutes in a fan oven), or until the cake has shrunk a little from the sides of the tin. Cool for about 10 minutes before turning it out on to a rack. Spread the top with the sieved and warmed marmalade, then coarsely grate the chocolate over the top. Without the topping, this cake keeps very well if carefully wrapped.

Royal Biscuits

100g (4oz) caster sugar
100g (4oz) butter
225g (8oz) flour
½ teaspoon baking powder
1 teaspoon ground cinnamon
1 egg
quince jelly
icing sugar

I make two versions of these, one flavoured with ginger and sandwiched with plum jam, and the other with cinnamon sandwiched with quince jelly. There are endless variations, but this is the basic recipe for my own favourite which is the cinnamon version.

Grease a baking sheet, and heat the oven to 170°C/350°F/ Gas 4. Cream the butter and sugar together until light. Mix in the beaten egg, then the flour sifted with the baking powder and cinnamon. Knead until smooth, turn on to a sparsely floured board and roll out thinly. Cut into circles with a biscuit cutter, then, with an apple corer, remove the centres from half the circles. Bake for about 15 minutes; cool on a rack. Spread the jelly on the whole biscuits, place the holed ones on top, then sift icing sugar over them.

Macaroons

225g (8oz) caster sugar
2 egg whites
150g (5oz) ground almonds
1 tablespoon cornflour
2 drops almond extract
rice paper
blanched almonds, split

Heat the oven to 170°C/350°F/Gas 4. Whisk the egg whites until frothy but not stiff. Mix together the ground almonds, cornflour and the sugar and beat this into the egg whites, together with the 2 drops (no more) of almond extract (not essence), until stiff. Leave to stand while you line a baking sheet with the rice paper, then put small spoonfuls on the rice paper, flattening each slightly; they will spread a little, so leave some space between each. Press a split almond on the top of each one, then bake for about 20 minutes, until a pale coffee colour.

Holiday Tea

Chudleighs and Scalded Cream
Strawberry Jam
Golden Syrup
Castlegate Fruit Cake
Strawberries

This is the kind of tea you might expect if you were arriving at *Holnicote*, *Lanhydrock* or *Knightshayes*, or any large country house in the West Country, for the holidays. Just such a tea was spread out for a working party arriving at the tea-room at *Watersmeet*, Devon, one hot July afternoon; we had walked over the hills to reach it, and more than did justice to it. If you live far from the West Country, the scalded or clotted cream will have to come by post, or from the supermarket. Round off this tea with fresh strawberries and more cream – if you think it can be managed.

Chudleighs

450g (1lb) strong plain flour
100g (4oz) butter
150ml (¼pt) milk
25g (1oz) fresh yeast or
    12g (½oz) dried
1 teaspoon each sugar and salt

Makes about twenty-four chudleighs.
Without wishing to start a local incident, I cannot find much difference between recipes for Devonshire Chudleighs and Cornish Splits. Both are soft white yeasty buns which are a perfect foil for lots of cream and jam or, if you are a Thunder and Lightning fan, lots of cream and golden syrup.

Make a yeast sponge as follows: warm the milk a little and add the yeast, stirring until it has dissolved and the milk is pale khaki, then add the sugar, salt and 4 tablespoons of the flour. Stir well, then leave to rise in a warm place until it begins to look bubbly and spongy. Put the butter in the same warm place so that it softens but does not melt. Add the butter and flour to the yeast sponge – if it is not very spongy, and flours do vary, add a little warm water – and knead to a silky, springy dough. Put the dough in a bowl and the bowl in a polythene bag, closing the top with a clothes peg. Leave to rise in the warm place for about 2 hours, until it has doubled in size. Heat the oven to 200°C/400°F/Gas 6. Punch the dough down and form into small balls about the size of a large egg and place them about 2·5cm (1in) apart on a greased baking sheet. Flatten the tops a little and bake them for 15–20 minutes until golden. Cover with a clean tea towel as they cool on a cake rack.

Strawberry Jam

1kg (2lb) strawberries
1kg (2lb) sugar-with-pectin

Recipes for Britain's most famous jam are legion, but this must be one of the simplest and quickest. Using one of the new blends of sugar-with-pectin, setting point is reached after not much more than 5 minutes, so that you lose none of the flavour and waste very little fruit.

Hull the strawberries, but do not wash them unless you feel you must. Slice them in half and put them in the preserving pan. Place over a low heat, mashing them with a wooden spoon; when the juice starts to run, add the sugar and stir until it has all dissolved. Raise the heat and bring to a full

rolling boil (which cannot be dispersed by stirring), and time for 4 minutes. Pull the pan off the heat and test by dropping a little jam on to a cold plate – if it wrinkles when pushed about, it is ready. Pot in warm, clean dry jars and cover.

Castlegate Fruit Cake

100g (4oz) plain flour
100g (4oz) wholemeal flour
1 teaspoon baking powder
pinch salt
225g (8oz) soft margarine
175g (6oz) soft brown sugar
50g (2oz) caster sugar
grated rind and juice 1 lemon
2 teaspoons mixed spice
3 large eggs
150g (5oz) each currants
  and sultanas
85g (3oz) raisins

A good light fruit cake, also excellent for expeditions to the beach or any other informal picnic, the lemony flavour is refreshing, the fruit element sustaining.

Grease and line a 26cm (10in) cake tin. Heat the oven to 160°C/325°F/Gas 3. Mix together the flours, baking powder, salt, spice and dried fruit. Cream the margarine with the sugars until fluffy, then add the eggs, one at a time, beating hard after each one has been added. Beat in the lemon rind, then fold in the flour/fruit mixture, finally adding the lemon juice and mixing well, but without beating any more. Spoon into the prepared tin and bake for about 2 hours, or until the cake has shrunk a little from the sides of the tin. Keeps well if hidden!

Nursery High Tea

Ramekins of Creamed Haddock with Toast Soldiers and Sailors
Chocolatey Weight-of-an-Egg Cakes
Cheese Bears

In memory of red-letter days at *Wightwick*, near Wolverhampton, this menu includes creamed haddock, but is given a more interesting treatment for the sophisticated 1990's child. The buns can be baked by children of any age, and so can the cheese bears. This also makes a good birthday tea, although you might prefer to swap the creamed haddock in favour of the filled roll recipes on pages 89–91.

Ramekins of Creamed Haddock with Toast Soldiers and Sailors

225g (8oz) undyed smoked
  haddock
450ml (¾pt) milk
60g (2½oz) butter
50g (2oz) flour
2 tablespoons tomato ketchup
1 egg, beaten
25g (1oz) grated Parmesan
  cheese

Makes four ramekins.
Cook the smoked haddock gently in the milk for about 10 minutes, or until it flakes easily. Drain it and reserve the milk. Cool, then meticulously remove all the skin and bones – evidence of either will put off any child. Grease 4 ramekins and heat the oven to 170°C/350°F/Gas 4. Make a sauce by melting the butter, stirring in the flour, and then the reserved milk. Cook until thick and smooth, then stir in the tomato ketchup and the finely broken-up haddock. Check the seasoning and stir in the beaten egg. Spoon into the ramekins and sprinkle with the Parmesan. Bake for 20 minutes, until puffy and golden. Allow to cook for a minute or two before serving, with soldiers and sailors – buttered white and brown toast, cut into fingers. For older children, use garlic butter on the sailors.

Chocolatey Weight-of-an-Egg Cakes

One egg, and its weight in:
caster sugar
soft margarine
self-raising flour
1 heaped tablespoon
  chocolate nibs
¼ teaspoon vanilla extract

Makes nine–ten cakes.
This is the 'take an egg and its weight in butter, flour and sugar' basic sponge cake mixture. Here it has chocolate nibs added and is baked in individual bun-tins, rather than as one large cake. I use a size 2 egg which weighs 70g (2½oz). Although the mixture only fills 9–10 bun tins, it can be doubled or trebled very easily.

Grease and flour a set of bun tins. Heat the oven to 170°C/350°F/Gas 4. Weigh the egg, make a note of the weight, then measure out that weight of margarine, sugar and flour. Cream the margarine and sugar, together with the vanilla extract. Add the beaten egg and beat well, then fold in the flour and add the chocolate nibs. Spoon into the bun tins and bake for about 20 minutes, until well risen and golden brown. Dust the icing sugar and eat as soon as they are cool.

Cheese Bears

175g (6oz) plain flour
85g (3oz) butter
100g (4oz) mature Cheddar
  cheese, grated
generous pinch salt
1 size 1 egg, separated
cold milk to mix
currants

For these you will need a bear-shaped biscuit cutter. If the children are adult in their tastes, use pieces of black olive or dried tomato for the eyes instead of currants.

Rub the butter into the flour until it looks like breadcrumbs, then stir in the cheese and salt. Add the beaten yolk, and enough cold milk to mix to a nice firm dough. Knead briefly and set aside in a cold place for about 30 minutes. Heat the oven to 200°C/400°F/Gas 6. Roll out the dough to 6mm ($\frac{1}{4}$in) thick, cut into bear shapes and arrange them about 1cm ($\frac{1}{2}$in) apart on a greased baking sheet. Beat the egg white until it is just liquid. Give the bears their currant eyes, then brush them all over with the egg white, and bake for about 10 minutes until they are a shiny golden brown. Cool on a rack.

CELEBRATING
CELEBRITIES

CELEBRATING CELEBRITIES

While working on this book I picked out events at National Trust properties which could be an excuse for a celebratory meal, simple or elaborate, intimate or ostentatious. But on several occasions I came across people who deserved something special in their honour, either for what they had achieved for the Trust itself, or for what they had achieved for the country in general, which made their bequest to the Trust especially valuable.

Accordingly, my first suggestion is a dinner in honour of a 'Lake District Supporters' Club'. At the head of the table would surely be Canon Hardwicke Rawnsley, one of the founders of the National Trust. He married into a prominent Cumberland family shortly after he was given the living of Wray, near Windermere, and later became a canon of Carlisle. Together with his wife Edith, and John Ruskin, who must also be present at this dinner, he was one of the chief promoters of the Keswick School of Industrial Art. Through his encouragement, Mrs Heelis, farmer and breeder of the famous local Herdwick sheep, better known south of Kendal as Beatrix Potter, the writer of children's books 'about yan rabbit', presented thousands of acres of fellside and farmland to the National Trust as part of her efforts to preserve this unique area. Also invited, although rather more in the spirit than the flesh, would be William and Dorothy Wordsworth, great inspirations to Hardwicke Rawnsley, and, going forward half a century, Dorothy Una Ratcliffe, who gave *Acorn Bank*, Cumbria, to the Trust and was a keen supporter of northern folk culture. This menu of local specialities is for them and all those who have done so much to preserve the Lake District.

A Lake District Dinner

Potted Char
Roast Saddle of Herdwick Lamb with Rowan Jelly
Clipping-time Pudding with Rum Butter

for eight

Potted Char

4 plump char, or trout, filleted
about 350g (12oz) butter
salt, freshly ground black pepper
pinch each allspice, mace and
    nutmeg

Char is a trout-like fish of great delicacy and infuriating elusiveness which lives in the deepest lakes and is fished for with special tackle. Potted char was one of the great gastronomic delights of the area in the nineteenth century and was dispatched round in the country in specially made char pots – shallow circular dishes decorated with a picture of the fish and with a groove round the top for the string which held the cover of waxed paper or cloth in place. As char is not easy to come by, trout will have to do instead. The method of cooking differs substantially from that for potted trout on page 87, and requires quantities of butter, although that is not eaten. The flavour is excellent and the butter, carefully removed, is delicious used for cooking fish at a later date.

Heat the oven to 140°C/275°F/Gas 1. Skin the fillets and rub them on both sides with a mixture of a little salt and the spices. Place the seasoned fillets in a shallow ovenproof dish and cover with the diced butter. Put in the oven and leave for about 20 minutes – until the butter has melted. Check that the melted butter completely covers the fish; if not, melt another few ounces in a saucepan and pour it over. Return the dish to the oven, cover it with its own lid or one made of foil, and continue to cook at the same temperature for 2½ hours. Take it out and cool completely. As soon as it is cold, store it in the fridge for up to a week before eating. To serve, carefully lift off the crust of butter (and store it in a covered jar in the fridge) and gently separate the fillets. Arrange each on a bed of watercress, with a wedge of lemon and brown bread-and-butter.

Roast Saddle of Herdwick Lamb

Herdwicks take longer to mature than other breeds, and may spend up to two years grazing the fells before being slaughtered. As a result, their meat is lean, close-grained and deliciously flavoured. Although the Trust is working hard to promote this breed outside their native area, their meat is not easy to obtain. The nearest alternative is to find a good butcher and buy a properly hung saddle from an autumn 'lamb'.

Roast the lamb as for the venison on page 31 in an oven preheated to 190°C/375°F/Gas 5, seasoning it well and putting it on a good bed of dried thyme sprigs and a few crushed juniper berries. When it is done, leave it to rest while you make the gravy by adding hot water and a good tablespoon of rowan jelly (see below) to the roasting tin, boiling it all up and straining it into a sauce boat.

Rowan Jelly

This jelly is the perfect partner to lamb and mutton, as it is less richly sweet than redcurrant jelly, with a subtle smoky, slightly tart flavour. Rowans grow happily anywhere there is a fairly acid, quick-draining soil. To make the jelly, half-fill a preserving pan with berries, washed and picked over to remove any leaves or woody bits of stalk. Add enough water for it to appear just underneath the top layer of berries, bring slowly to the boil, then simmer gently until the berries pop and begin to soften. When quite soft, tip the contents of the pan into a jelly bag and leave to drain for several hours, or overnight. Next day, measure the juice and add 450g (1lb) granulated or preserving sugar to each 600ml (1pt) juice. Place over a low heat until the sugar dissolves, then raise the heat and boil rapidly until setting point is reached – about 30 minutes. This jelly never sets firmly, which is why most recipes suggest adding apples. But they do alter the unique flavour of the rowans, and a soft set is an advantage in a jelly which is more often added to sauces than balanced on a piece of bread.

Clipping-time Pudding

100g (4oz) short-grain
    pudding rice
1·2l (2pt) creamy milk
50g (2oz) sugar
strip lemon peel
½ teaspoon cinnamon
100g (4oz) raisins
1 egg
40g (1½oz) unsalted butter

This is an embellished rice pudding, once made in great quantities and served at the suppers given to the groups of shearers who came to shear the Herdwicks' wiry fleeces. Some recipes included bone marrow to enrich it, others butter, cream or eggs; this one uses butter and an egg. If you serve it cold, as it was at those shearing suppers, then cream is the best accompaniment, but I think it better still served warm with another Cumbrian delicacy, rum butter, melting aromatically into the creaminess of the rice.

Put the rice in a small pan and cover with cold water. Bring to the boil, leave it to boil while you slowly count to ten, then drain and rinse. Put it into a heavy pan with the milk, sugar, lemon peel, cinnamon and raisins and simmer gently until the rice is cooked – about 25–30 minutes. Draw off the heat. Heat the oven to 170°C/350°F/Gas 4. Whisk the egg, then beat this and the butter into the rice and spoon into a souffle dish. Bake for about 20 minutes, until puffy and golden.

Rum butter

225g (8oz) unsalted butter
175g (6oz) soft brown sugar
6 tablespoons dark rum
generous grating of nutmeg

This is a useful standby to spread on crumpets for tea, to fill a chocolate cake, or to spoon on to baked apples, apple pie or apple crumble, so it is worth making more than is needed here, and storing it in the fridge or freezer.

Melt the butter over a low heat. Draw off the heat and stir in the rum, sugar and nutmeg. Leave it to cool, beating it hard every so often to blend the ingredients. When cold and well mixed, spoon into a decorative pot if using immediately, or into a small plastic container with a lid to store in fridge or freezer.

Ferguson's Gang's Feast

Lobster Cutlets
Potato Salad
Raspberry Cream and Fresh Pineapple

for eight

It is impossible, to this day, to name the guests at this feast, since none of this elusive band of conservationists has revealed his or her identity. They are known in National Trust history only by their nicknames: Sister Agatha, See Mee Run, the Artichoke, Bill Stickers, His Bloodiness the Bishop, Shot Biddy, Red Biddy, and several more. Their contributions to the Trust in the mid-1930s included *Shalford Mill*, on the Tillingbourne in Surrey, *Newtown Town Hall* on the Isle of Wight and the ruins of *Steventon Priory*, near Abingdon, as well as land along the Cornish coast and bags of loot. Their methods were wildly unorthodox, with melodramatic cloak-and-dagger tactics that involved the delivery of £100 in silver coins to the Trust headquarters by a masked woman, secret meetings at Shalford Mill around one of the millstones, donations sent wrapped round cigars or in throat pastille packets. They shared a love of good food and wine. 'A typical meal', wrote Sarah-Jane Forder in her carefully opaque article on the Gang in the National Trust *Magazine*, 'would consist of lobster cutlets accompanied by potato salad and followed by raspberry cream and fresh pineapple'. Here are the recipes for this menu – the quantities are for eight since that was the number which could be seated in comfort around the Shalford Mill millstone.

Lobster Cutlets

*1 cooked lobster, weighing
   about 450g (1lb)
450g (1lb) very fresh whte fish,
   skinned and boned
2 tablespoons finely chopped
   parsley
25g (1oz) potato or cornflour
1 large egg
1 dessertspoon anchovy essence
1 tablespoon lemon juice
½ teaspoon Tabasco or
   large pinch cayenne
groundnut oil for frying
seasoned semolina*

These used to be made by adding the shellfish to a thick floury sauce which then set firm and could be cut into shapes. This kind of mixture can be difficult to deal with, and needs to be left to set for about 12 hours. This recipe is in the modern mode, easier, quicker, lighter and better-flavoured.

Remove all the meat from the lobster, not forgetting the claws, and the coral if it is a hen lobster, and put it in a food processor. Add all the other ingredients except the last two and process until finely chopped and well blended. Chill for about an hour in the fridge, then form into 24 small flat cakes. Dip into the seasoned semolina (this gives a nice crunchy texture), shake off the surplus, and fry for about 3 minutes on each side over a medium heat. Drain on kitchen paper and serve either hot or cold. They are particularly good partnered by the avocado dip on page 93, as well as the potato salad which follows.

Potato Salad

*1 kg (2¼lb) waxy potatoes –
   Desirée, La Ratte or Charlotte
1 bunch spring onions
2 tablespoons pimento-stuffed
   olives, finely sliced*

FOR THE MAYONNAISE

*1 whole egg
1 egg yolk
1 tablespoon lemon juice
about 300ml (½pt) light
   olive oil
salt and pepper*

Boil the potatoes in their skins. Skin and slice the potatoes while they are still warm. Make the mayonnaise in the blender or processor – put in the egg and egg yolk and a tablespoonful of the oil and blend for 30 seconds. With the motor still running, add the rest of the oil in a thin stream through the funnel in the lid until the mixture reaches the consistency of thick cream. Add the lemon juice, salt and pepper to taste. Fold the potatoes into this, together with the finely chopped spring onions, and scatter the olive slices over the top.

Raspberry Cream and Fresh Pineapple

Use the recipe for raspberry mousse (page 108) to fill a hollowed-out pineapple (to appeal to the Gang's sense of disguise), serving the pineapple flesh, diced and doused with *eau-de-vie de framboise*, or other liqueur, as an accompaniment.

Thomas Hardy's Carol-Singing Supper

Ham and Potato Bake
Dorset Apple Cake
Mulled Cider

for twelve

For the festive season, a carol-singing supper for Thomas Hardy, to be held in the cottage at *Higher Bockhampton*, near Dorchester, where he spent his boyhood and which is now owned by the Trust. Just such an event is described in *Under the Greenwood Tree*, to honour the 'greatest of English country writers', as L. A. G. Strong described him in his portrait of Hardy. This description, one of the *Sixteen Portraits* edited by Strong and published by the National Trust in 1951, ends 'There is no writer whose house meant more to his life and writing, none therefore which his country should be at greater pains to keep as he left it.'

Ham and Potato Bake

1·4kg (3lb) cooked joint
  of collar bacon
3 large mild onions, sliced
2kg (4½lb) potatoes, peeled
  and thickly sliced
ham or bacon stock
225g (8oz) mature Cheddar
  cheese, grated
2 thick slices brown bread
soft butter
mustard
2 teaspoons dried sage

'Mrs Dewy sat in a brown settle by the side of the glowing wood fire – so glowing that with a doubting compression of the lips she would now and then rise and put her hand upon the hams and flitches of bacon lining the chimney, to reassure herself that they were not being broiled instead of smoked – a misfortune that had been known to happen at Christmas-time.'

Dice the bacon and layer it with the onions and potatoes in a deep ovenproof dish, seasoning each layer with a little salt, plenty of pepper and a sprinkling of the sage. Finish with a layer of potatoes. Pour in the stock to come level with the top layer. Butter the slices of bread, spread them with a thin layer of mustard, cut into cubes and then reduce them to breadcrumbs in a blender or processor. Mix with the grated cheese, and then sprinkle this mixture over the top. Bake in a moderate oven (160°C/325°F/Gas 3) until the potatoes are soft and the top crisp and savoury – about an hour. To make

145

a richer and more filling dish, make a sauce (melt 60g/2½oz butter, stir in 50g/2oz flour, then slowly add 1·2l/2pt hot stock and cook until smooth) and layer the ingredients with this instead of the stock.

Dorset Apple Cake

550g (1¼lb) cooking apples, peeled, cored and chopped
450g (1lb) flour
225g (8oz) golden granulated sugar
225g (8oz) butter
3 teaspoons baking powder
pinch ground cloves
milk to mix

Line a roasting tin with baking parchment. Heat the oven to 160°C/350°F/Gas 4. Rub the butter into the flour, then stir in the baking powder, cloves, apples and sugar, using your hands to make sure everything is well mixed together. Add enough milk to make a firm dough, then spread it evenly in the roasting tin. Bake for about 45 minutes, until golden brown. Turn out on to a rack, cut into squares and serve warm, with cream.

Mulled Cider

2·5l (4pt) medium dry cider
2 well-flavoured eating apples
4 cloves
2 x 10cm (4in) cinnamon sticks
175g (6oz) demerara sugar

'"This in the cask here is a drop o' the right sort" (tapping the cask); "'tis a real drop o' cordial from the best picked apples".'

Score the skin of the apples round the middle and bake them for about 30 minutes, or until soft. Stick the cloves in the apples. Put the cider in a large pan with the clove-stuck apples and cinnamon sticks, and bring slowly to just below boiling point. Reduce the heat so the mixture does not boil and stir in the sugar until dissolved. Keep hot, but make sure it never boils.

A Centenary Picnic Lunch for the Founding Trio

Tomato Consommé with Sherry
Mutton Pies
Rabbit Terrine
Smoked Fish in Aspic
Lettuce Hearts in a Tarragon Cream Dressing
Potato Salad with Marjoram
Spiced Prune Relish
Cheesecakes
Fresh Seasonal Fruit
Potted Cheeses and Celery Cream Crackers
Elderflower Cordial
Mineral Water
Chilled rosé or a light red wine
Coffee

for eight

And finally, as the ultimate celebration of the National Trust's Centenary, a picnic lunch on Box Hill, Surrey, for the founding trio. It was on 12 January 1895 that several years of hard work and thought on the part of three people – Octavia Hill, Robert Hunter and Hardwicke Rawnsley – culminated in the official formation of The National Trust for Places of Historic Interest or Natural Beauty.

Of the three, Robert Hunter has the closest connection with Box Hill. While living near Haslemere he began working to preserve the parts of Surrey threatened by the newly-expanding railway network, particularly the south-facing slopes of the North Downs so easily reached by Londoners. The preservation of Box Hill occupied him up to his death in 1913, and it must have comforted him in his very last days to know that the cost of buying the 230 acres was to be met by Leopold Salomons.

This beautiful stretch of downland admirably embodies the ideals of both Hunter – who had brought his experience as honorary solicitor to the Commons Preservation Society to the founding of the National Trust – and Octavia Hill – whose aim was to provide 'open air sitting-rooms for the poor'. Now, as then, it fulfils her dream of 'a bit of green hilly ground near a city, where fresh winds may blow, and

where wild flowers are still found, and where happy people can still walk within reach of their home'.

I don't suggest this picnic for the exact date of the National Trust's birthday: January can be very chilly on Box Hill even for the hardiest picnicker. But it is ideal for a warm July Sunday, when a hot drive out of London is rewarded by the sight of the wooded slopes punctuated with the darker green of yew and holly and, of course, the box which gives the beauty spot its name.

Nothing in this menu, except the salads, needs much last minute attention, so preparations can start well in advance. The spiced prunes can be made up to a fortnight before you need them, and the rabbit terrine will keep for a week in the fridge. The potted cheeses, and the cream crackers, if carefully stored, keep well too. The cheesecake can be frozen. So can the mutton pies, at a pinch. The smoked fish in aspic will keep for two days in the fridge and so will the consommé.

Tomato Consommé with Sherry

2 x 295g (10½oz) tins condensed
    beef consommé
1 x 400g (14oz) tin chopped
    tomatoes
bayleaf
clove garlic, lightly crushed
    (optional)
generous sherry glass medium
    dry sherry
squeeze lemon juice

A very easy recipe, which can be served hot if the day is cold, or chilled.

Dilute the tins of condensed beef consommé as directed on the label and put in a saucepan together with the chopped tomatoes, the bayleaf, and garlic if you are using it. Bring slowly to a simmer, stirring from time to time, then put a lid on the pan, withdraw from the heat and leave to infuse for 30 minutes. Strain the consommé into a clean pan and add the sherry, stir well then add a squeeze of lemon juice to lift the flavour a little. Either chill and pour into a thermos which you have left in the fridge for an hour or so, or reheat and pour into a thermos rinsed out with boiling water. Take some small ready-buttered granary rolls to serve with this.

Mutton Pies

SHORTCRUST PASTRY

350g (12oz) plain flour
75g (3oz) butter
75g (3oz) lard
½ teaspoon dried thyme
salt and pepper
chilled milk to mix

FOR THE FILLING

1 blade-end joint of shoulder of
* lamb or mutton, weighing*
* about 900g (2lb)*
2 small onions
2 cloves
bouquet garni – parsley, strip
* lemon peel, plenty of thyme*
* and marjoram, tied in a*
* bundle*
1 large carrot, split
6 peppercorns
salt
75g (3oz) finely chopped
* mushrooms*
15g (½oz) butter
1 tablespoon flour
2 teaspoons finely chopped fresh
* marjoram*
freshly ground pepper, salt
4 large tablespoons redcurrant
* jelly, to glaze*

If you are lucky enough to be able to get real mutton, then you will be able to sample these Victorian delicacies at their very best. Most of us, however, will have to make do with lamb which has just reached adulthood. Whichever you use, it is best to cook the meat specially for this recipe, rather than just use up cold meat from a joint of roast lamb. Cook the mutton or lamb the day before you make the pies.

Peel one of the onions and stick the cloves in it. Put it in a large pan with the meat, bouquet garni, carrot, the pepper-corns and a dessertspoonful of salt. Cover with cold water and bring slowly to the boil. Skim off any froth which rises to the surface, lower the heat, cover the pan and simmer gently for 30 minutes per 450g (1lb) weight of meat, plus 20 minutes. Leave to cool in the liquid until next day. Remove from the liquid and finely dice 450g (1lb) of the leanest meat. Melt the butter in a heavy pan, add the remaining onion, finely chopped, and a sprinkling of salt and let it cook until just beginning to brown. Add the mushrooms and cook a minute or two longer. Then stir in the flour and, off the heat, about 150ml (¼ pint) of the stock in which the lamb cooked. Return to the heat and stir until thickened. Add the lamb, the marjoram, and seasoning to taste. As these pies are to be eaten cold they should be fairly highly seasoned. Leave to cool. Make up the pastry: mix the flour, thyme and season-ing together, then rub in the fats until finely blended; add enough chilled milk to mix to a firm dough. Knead briefly, wrap in greaseproof paper and leave to rest for an hour or so.

Roll out two-thirds of the pastry and use it to line 12 greased deep bun tins. Put a generous amount of filling in each. Roll out the remaining pastry, cut out lids and brush each with a little cold water to help bond them to the bases, pinching tops and bottoms together. Cut a small cross in the top of each. Bake in a moderate oven (190°C/375°G/Gas 5) for about 20 minutes. Take out and remove carefully from the tins. In a small pan, melt the redcurrant jelly until just runny. Brush this over the lids of the warm pies and leave to get cold. Serve with the potato salad and spiced prune relish.

Rabbit Terrine

about 700g (1½lb) rabbit, to yield about 450g (1lb) boneless meat

450g (1lb) boneless fat shoulder pork

6–8 thin rashers of unsmoked streaky bacon

2 tablespoons finely chopped fresh marjoram

1 tablespoon finely chopped fresh parsley

1 small clove garlic

6 crushed juniper berries

1 wineglass medium dry white wine

2 tablespoons brandy

salt and freshly ground pepper

pinch nutmeg

generous sprig fresh thyme

This terrine is flavoured with thyme and marjoram, to echo the plants which form part of the diet of the Box Hill rabbits. If you can get wild rabbit, so much the better, but make sure it is a young one or it could be very tough. To avoid dryness it is important to use a piece of pork with plenty of fat as the rabbit yields none.

Mince or chop the rabbit meat coarsely and put in a large bowl. Treat the pork in the same way and add to the rabbit. If you do have a piece of pork with the skin on, reserve this and use it to cover the terrine before putting on the lid. Crush the peeled garlic clove to a paste with 3 teaspoons of salt and add it to the meats, together with the herbs, juniper berries, white wine and brandy, a generous grinding of pepper and the nutmeg. Mix thoroughly – using your hands is best. Cover and leave to stand for about an hour in a cool place. Stretch each rasher of bacon to about twice its length, using a heavy knife as an 'iron'. Place the thyme artistically at the bottom of an oval or oblong ovenproof dish, about 10–13cm (4–5in) deep and 21–23cm (8–9in) long (when you turn the terrine out onto a dish the thyme should form a decoration). On top of the thyme arrange the bacon rashers so that they line the base and sides with a little left to fold over the top. Pile the terrine mixture carefully into the dish, making sure there are no air pockets, but without pressing it down too much. Fold the ends of the rashers over the top and add any pork rind available, fat side down. Cover the dish with its lid, if it has one, or a lid of greaseproof paper and then one of foil if it does not. Stand it in a roasting tin and add boiling water from the kettle to come about one-third of the way up the sides of the dish. Put in a low oven, set at 160°C/325°F/Gas 3, to cook for 1½ hours, removing the lid for the final 20 minutes. The meat will have shrunk away from the sides of the dish and the gap be filled with delicious juices which will set to an equally delicious jelly.

Turn the terrine out on to a suitably decorative plate, having first dipped the base in a bowl of very hot water and counted slowly to five. To transport it to the picnic, wash

and dry the dish in which it was cooked, then put it over the terrine, holding it firmly in place with a shroud of cling film. Serve in generous slices with the potato and marjoram salad and the spiced prune relish.

Smoked Fish in Aspic

450g (1lb) undyed smoked haddock
225g (8oz) smoked trout
225g (8oz) smoked salmon trimmings
50–75g (2–3oz) frozen prawns
5 tablespoons crème fraîche
1 or 2 bayleaves
1 tablespoon finely chopped parsley
1 dessertspoon finely chopped tarragon
2 packets aspic jelly powder
pepper and a little salt
few drops of Tabasco
approx. 1 tablespoon lemon juice

Poach the haddock in water to cover, plus a bayleaf or two, for about 15 minutes or until tender. Cool, remove the skin and bones and flake. Mix with the herbs. Mix the smoked trout with the crème fraîche in a food processor to a coarse purée and season with a little salt if necessary plus a few drops of Tabasco to sharpen it. Cut the smoked salmon trimmings into strips and moisten with a little lemon juice. Make up the aspic jelly powder according to the instructions on the packet, adding a squeeze of lemon juice. Pour a thin film of aspic over the base of a decorative bowl from which the smoked fish will be served and allow it to set. Then layer the three fish mixtures, beginning with the haddock, then some of the smoked trout cream, then strips of smoked salmon. Finish with a layer of smoked haddock and smooth the top as much as possible. Arrange the defrosted prawns in a pattern on the top. Pour about 600ml (1pt) of the just-beginning-to-set aspic mixture gently over the contents of the dish and leave it to set in the fridge. When chilled, remelt the remaining aspic over a low heat and pour enough over the surface of the dish to glaze it attractively. Refrigerate until needed. Serve with the lettuce heart salad.

Lettuce Hearts in a Tarragon Cream Dressing

Cut four Little Gem lettuce hearts into quarters, rinse them and pat them dry and pack in a plastic box. Take the following dressing separately in a screw-top jar, so everyone can help themselves. Mix a tub of crème fraîche with a dessertspoonful of tarragon vinegar, salt and freshly ground pepper and a tablespoonful of chopped fresh tarragon.

Potato Salad with Marjoram

Scrape abut 900g (2lb) of new potatoes and cook in well-salted boiling water until done. Drain and return to the hot pan to dry off a little. Have ready a vinaigrette made with good olive oil and white wine vinegar in the usual proportions – 1 of vinegar to 6 of oil – season it well and toss the potatoes in it while they are still warm. Add a liberal amount of chopped fresh marjoram and mix again.

Spiced Prune Relish

685g (1½lb) no-soak prunes
450ml (¾pt) water
5 tablespoons red wine vinegar
100g (4oz) muscovado sugar
1 cinnamon stick, broken in half
8 cloves
6 allspice berries
3 blades of mace (or ½ teaspoon
  powdered mace)
piece of whole nutmeg (or ½
  teaspoon powdered nutmeg)
bayleaf

Put all the ingredients in a heavy pan and bring very slowly to a gentle simmer. When the sugar has melted, check that the liquid just covers the prunes – if it doesn't, add a little more water. Put a lid on the pan and cook very gently until the prunes are tender, about 20 minutes. Lift the prunes from the syrup and put them in a jar with a good lid, and boil the liquid in the pan until syrupy and reduced by about half. Cool a little then pour over the prunes and screw on the lid. These are best made at least a week in advance; they keep well and are delicious with all sorts of cold meat and game.

Cheesecakes

85g (3oz) unsalted butter
125g (4oz) caster sugar
150g (5oz) cottage cheese
150g (5oz) cream cheese
grated rind of 1 lemon
2 eggs, separated
85g (3oz) ground almonds
½ teaspoon vanilla extract

These cheesecakes are the old-fashioned sort, baked without a crumb base in individual ramekins, so they are light in texture and easily transported; if you prefer you can make one large one (in a lined 20cm (8in) cake tin with a loose base) and cut it into slices. Serve with any fresh fruit, especially strawberries and raspberries, and some single cream to pour over.

Beat together the butter, sugar and lemon rind until pale and creamy, then add the egg yolks and beat well. Mix in the cheeses and the vanilla extract until well blended, and fold in the ground almonds. Whip the egg whites until stiff and fold into the mixture. Spoon into the greased ramekins or lined cake tin and bake at 175°C/350°F/Gas 4 for 20–25

minutes for the individual cheesecakes, and about double that time for the large one. Switch off the oven when done and leave the cheesecakes in the oven until completely cold.

Potted Cheeses

Not just a canny way to use up odds and ends of cheese, these two recipes are good in their own right. The first is Edwardian with a bit of a kick; the second, milder and creamier, dates from the eighteenth century.

EDWARDIAN POTTED CHEESE

225g (8oz) mature Cheddar
   cheese
85g (3oz) unsalted butter
1 teaspoon English mustard
1 tablespoon chilli vinegar (or
   white wine vinegar and
   Tabasco)
12 walnut halves

Put the first four ingredients in the processor or blender and mix to a paste. Add the walnuts and continue to process just enough to break them into little bits, but not so much that they lose their identity. Spoon into a small pot and smooth the top. Cover with foil and keep in the fridge until needed.

GEORGIAN POTTED CHEESE

225g (8oz) best Cheshire cheese
50g (2oz) slightly salted butter
3 tablespoons medium dry
   sherry
2 large pinches powdered mace

Put all the ingredients in the processor or blender and mix to a smooth paste. Pot and store as above.

Celery Cream Crackers

225g (8oz) plain flour
50g (2oz) salted butter
90ml (approx. 6 tablespoons)
   single cream
1 teaspoon baking powder
1 tablespoon culinary celery
   seed
½ teaspoon salt
cold water to mix

These are delicious and very easy to make. The celery seed flavouring is extra good with cheese, but it is optional and you can substitute poppy or sesame seeds if you prefer, or leave the crackers plain.

Mix together the flour, baking powder, salt and celery seed, then rub in the butter until the texture of ground almonds. Add the cream, and just enough cold water to make a firm dough. Knead the dough briefly and then leave to rest for a

few minutes. Preheat the oven to 160°C/330°F/Gas 3. Flour a board and rolling pin lightly and roll out the dough as thinly as possible. Cut into large rounds, prick each all over with a fork in a spiral pattern and arrange on a greased baking sheet. Bake for about 18–20 minutes, less in a fan oven, until pale gold. Cool on a rack and store in an airtight plastic box where they will keep well for up to a week.

Elderflower Cordial

10–12 heads fresh elderflowers
685g (1½lb) caster sugar
25g (1oz) citric acid (optional)
rind and juice of 1 lemon
600ml (1pt) boiling water

Quite possibly the formidable Octavia Hill would not have approved of alcoholic liquor at a picnic lunch, but even she could not have found fault with a refreshing glass of elderflower cordial. This is now widely available, but is much cheaper to make at home when elderflowers are in season. If you include the optional citric acid it will keep longer.

Check the elderflowers for any insects by shaking them over a bowl of water. Put the flowers, sugar, citric acid (if using) and the lemon rind and juice into a large bowl or jug and pour over the boiling water. Stir well, cover with a plate, and leave to cool overnight. Next day strain through a coffee filter, or a sieve lined with a clean J-cloth, and bottle. Dilute to taste with still or sparkling mineral water and, on festive occasions, garnish each glass with a leaf or two of mint.

The best way to serve coffee at a picnic seems to be to take a jar of high-class instant (such as Alta Rica or Cap Colombie) plus thermoses of very hot water, rather than thermoses of ready-made coffee which tastes pretty awful after several hours in a flask. Take pouring cream, and brown sugar lumps which are much easier to deal with than loose sugar. And remember to take chocolate – as many types as possible – it is rarely refused.

RECIPE INDEX

PEOPLE AND PLACES INDEX